Chivalry & Command

500 YEARS OF HORSE GUARDS

OSPREY
PUBLISHING

Chivalry & Command

500 YEARS OF HORSE GUARDS

BRIAN HARWOOD

First published in Great Britain in 2006 by Osprey Publishing,
Midland House, West Way, Botley, Oxford OX2 0PH, United Kingdom.
443 Park Avenue South, New York, NY 10016, USA.
Email: info@ospreypublishing.com

A CIP catalogue record for this book is available from the British Library

ISBN-10: 1 84603 109 5
ISBN-13: 978 1 84603 109 0

Brian Harwood has asserted his right under the Copyright, Designs and Patents Act, 1988, to be identified as the author of this book.

Page layout by Ken Vail Graphic Design, Cambridge, UK
Index by David and Alison Worthington
Typeset in Sabon, ITC Stone Serif, Trajan, Truesdell and Minion
Maps by The Map Studio Ltd
Originated by United Graphics Pte Ltd, Singapore
Printed and bound in China through Worldprint Ltd

06 07 08 09 10   10 9 8 7 6 5 4 3 2 1

For a catalogue of all books published by Osprey please contact:

NORTH AMERICA
Osprey Direct c/o Random House Distribution Center, 400 Hahn Road, Westminster, MD 21157, USA
E-mail: info@ospreydirect.com

ALL OTHER REGIONS
Osprey Direct UK, P.O. Box 140, Wellingborough, Northants, NN8 2FA, UK
E-mail: info@ospreydirect.co.uk
www.ospreypublishing.com

Front cover: photo by Dean Ryan
Back cover: Topfoto
Title page: The new Horse Guards viewed through the old Tudor Court Gate of Whitehall Palace c.1763. The depicted 1530s gateway with its brickwork Stuart additions was the reason why the Horse Guards building came to be where it is – directly opposite the state entrance to the monarch's official London residence. At this date the mounted guards are still 'Private Gentlemen' from the Troops of Horse Guards; in 1788 it all changed when these Troops were converted to two regular Household Cavalry regiments of Life Guards. The sentries in the courtyard appear, from their mitre headdress, to belong to the Horse Grenadier Guards; they were later reformed as Household Cavalry in 1788. (E. Rooker, author's collection)
Inside covers: The Victorian army administration at Horse Guards in 1847. At a period of maximum empire expansion, the ground and first-floor plans of Barry's proposed rebuild show clearly the myriad departments, both military and civil, competing for space within Horse Guards. In the north wing of the ground floor are the stalls allocated to the War Office Letter Party, denoted as being for the 'Light Horse'. In contrast the Household Cavalry was defined as being a 'Heavy Horse' regiment. These 'Letter Party' stalls survive today. The next floor over the 'principal' one shown was a similar honeycomb warren of offices, while for the next floor over that, and the attic storey above (comprising 68 rooms), Barry designated for each, 'The whole of the rooms … are proposed to be appropriated to subordinate offices and depots for papers and also the domestic accommodation of the House Keepers, Office Keepers and Messengers'. (TNA (PRO), WORK 30/186–7)

Abbreviations

CSP Dom.	Calendar of State Papers Domestic
CTB	Calendar of Treasury Books
CTP	Calendar of Treasury Papers
CVA	Calendar of Venetian Archives
E	Exchequer Records
HMC	Historic Manuscripts Commission Reports
HO	Home Office Papers
L&P H. VIII	Letters and Papers Henry VIII
LC	Lord Chamberlain's Records
LCC	London County Council
LR	Land Revenue Auditors
LRRO	Land Revenue Records Office
NAM	National Army Museum
PRO	Public Record Office
SP	State Paper Office
T	Treasury Records
WAR	War Office
WORK	Ministry of Public Building and Works

Contents

Acknowledgements

As a London attraction, Horse Guards receives hundreds of thousands of visitors each year: it appears on every tourist's 'must see' list. However, most visitors to Horse Guards have little or no inkling of the rich history, relative to both the nation and to Whitehall, that this building conceals, and as an institution, it is familiar only to those who work within its unique environment. In what follows, the variety of patterns that illuminate this history – military, political, architectural, social and ceremonial – will, era by era, reveal to the reader how the Horse Guards story is inextricably interwoven with recurring themes of national importance, all played out in the Whitehall arena. The study of Horse Guards is, therefore, the study of Whitehall: one begets the other.

Prior to this book, the only other published account of Horse Guards existed within the massive volumes of the old London County Council (LCC) *Survey of London*, published in the 1930s. However, the LCC Survey's account of Horse Guards (Vol. XVI pp.5–16) provides landmark coverage rather than detailed historical presentation: constraints of editorial brevity necessarily applied as the Survey pursued its aim to historically plot the lives of all central London buildings. Also, the Survey is only to be found in a few specialist reference libraries, and these mostly in London. The need for an accessible historical account of Horse Guards is long overdue: it is hoped this work satisfies that need.

In following the routes necessary to build on the LCC Survey highlights, I remain acutely aware that I am treading along many ways essentially unexplored, thus the conclusions I have arrived at from previously unknown or unused documentary sources remain mine and mine alone. This is not to say advice has not been sought from others better qualified in specialist areas – as acknowledged below – indeed, it is hoped that readers may offer new viewpoints on the documented references cited. Perhaps this work might also serve as a starting point encouraging others to expand upon the variety of historical themes that go to make up the Horse Guards story. Of necessity, some features of the regimental histories of the Guards regiments merge with the Horse Guards story: I apologize if in any instance I have involuntarily erred in the detail of those histories.

This account having been some decades in research and gestation, I have inevitably drawn upon the resources of a multitude of institutions and individuals, both in the UK and overseas; consequently, an exhaustive listing of contributors is impossible to compile. I hope this work suitably reflects all their collective efforts. However, I feel the following must not escape especial mention: First and foremost, the Household Cavalry Museum, in close conjunction with the Guards Museum. Regimental Headquarters (RHQ) Household Cavalry; Headquarters London District; Household Division Funds; Records Office, Grenadier Guards; Records Office, Coldstream Guards; Records Office, Scots Guards; Home Headquarters, The Queen's Royal Lancers; The Mountbatten Memorial Trust; National Army Museum; Imperial War Museum; Museum of London; Corporation of London Guildhall Museum; British Museum; English Heritage, National Monuments Record and Government Historic Estates Unit; St John's College, Oxford; St Catherine's College, Oxford; Worcester College, Oxford; Pepysian Library, Magdalene College, Cambridge; Library of the Freemason's Hall; Historic Manuscripts Commission; Public Record Office, Kew; The British Library; Home Office Library; Ministry of Defence Library; National Gallery; Royal Institute of British Architects; Royal Library, Windsor Castle; Royal Library, St James's Palace; Royal United Service Institution; Sir John Soane's Museum; The Society for Army Historical Research; General Editor, *Survey of London*; Treasury Library; Victoria and Albert Museum; Wellington Museum, Apsley House; Westminster City Libraries; The Army Museums' Ogilby Trust; Countess of Berkeley; Lord Sackville; The Duke of Devonshire's Library, Chatsworth; Leeds University, School of History; John Rylands Library; Dorset County Record Office; *Country Life*; Museum of Leathercraft; Castle Museum, Nottingham; Goldsmiths' Hall; Whitechapel Bell Foundry; Thwaites & Reed, Clockmakers; The Parker Gallery; Biblioteca Nacional de Lisboa; National Register of Archives (Scotland); Surrey County Record Office; Scottish United Services Museum; Antiquarian Horological Society; Hampshire County Council; Kent County Record Office, Brasted Place, Kent; Dover Castle; Gloucestershire County Records Office; Hampton Court Palace; Tate Gallery; National Gallery; National Portrait Gallery; Royal Academy of Arts; The College of Arms; Wallace Collection; Shropshire Record Office; Museo Accademia, Venice; Government Art Collection; *Illustrated London News*; Reuters; *Daily Mirror*; Mellon Art Collection; Acadia University, Nova Scotia; Rijksmuseum, Amsterdam; Academie d'Architecture, Paris; Bibliotheque Publique et Universitaire, Geneva; and Defense Attaché Office, American Embassy, London. Last but not in any way least, I must wholeheartedly thank the team members at Osprey who have guided this work through to its final fruition, and amongst whom I must highlight the sustained dedication of Development Editor Ruth Sheppard. Her skilful piloting of my literary efforts around the perils of the previously uncharted research waters in which I chose to delve, demonstrated a professional skill of the highest order.

BUCKINGHAM PALACE

As Colonel of The Blues and Royals, I am pleased to welcome this history of a site universally identified with the Household Cavalry, which has also witnessed so many of the defining moments in British history in both war and peacetime.

For five centuries Horse Guards has been associated with the men and women who guard this country, and this book is a fitting tribute to the soldiers who have mounted guard there and continue to do so every day. I know that it will be of particular interest to students of British history and architecture, and all those visiting the beautiful surroundings of Horse Guards and Whitehall.

HRH The Princess Royal

Chronology

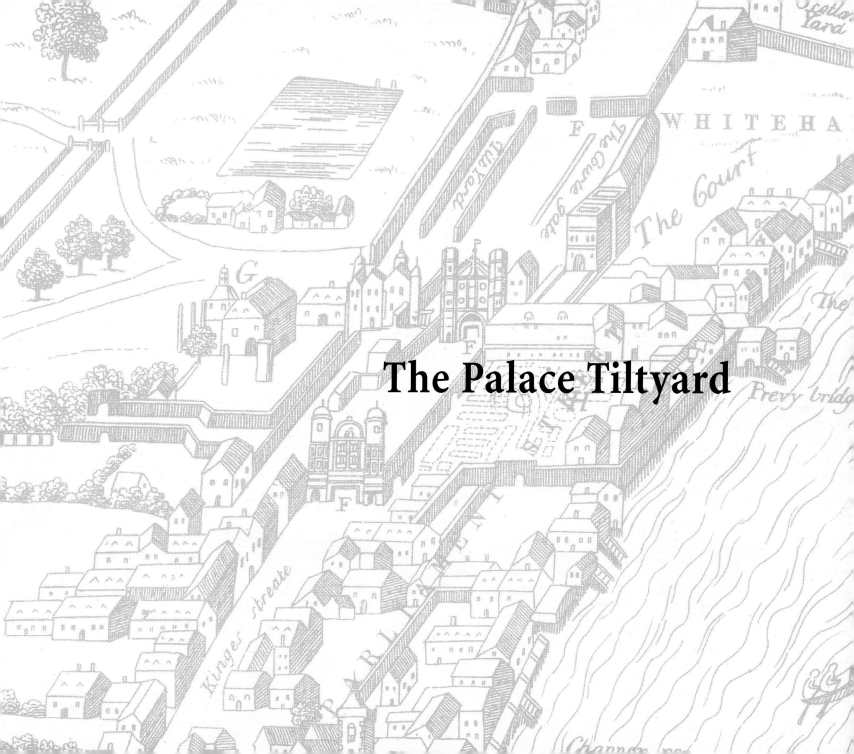

The Palace Tiltyard

'Tis now the King's and called Whitehall'

The history of Horse Guards begins in the 16th century at York Place, the luxurious London palace of the archbishops of York. Sprawled along the east side of King Street – the main thoroughfare leading from Westminster via 'Charrynge Crosse' to the City around St Paul's – York Place had stood there since 1245. Until Tudor times, the area had remained relatively rural, the Thameside locality at York Place still sometimes called by its colloquial Saxon name 'Enedehithe', meaning 'sea bird shore'. Covering much of the land between the Thames and King Street, the episcopal palace stretched south from Scotland Yard for almost a quarter of a mile towards Westminster. Its main gateway stood opposite the houses on the future Horse Guards site, astride a public road leading down to a very ancient landing stage and ferry point: a road now covered by Horse Guards Avenue. Westminster Palace to the south had clustered around the abbey since the time of Edward the Confessor, but over the centuries had been prone to flood and fire damage; some kings in the past had temporarily lodged in York Place while Westminster was made habitable again. By the 1520s, a total of 24 successive archbishops of York, including three cardinals, had combined their efforts to create for themselves the most opulent palace in London.

Destined to be the last incumbent of York Place, the ostentatious Cardinal Wolsey, with his sumptuous finery of office, often outshone even his king, Henry VIII (r.1509–47). The disgruntled Venetian ambassador, Guistinian, summarized the cardinal's extravagance for his masters:

He is the person who rules both the king and the entire kingdom. No one obtains audience from him unless at the third or fourth attempt. I had to traverse eight rooms before reaching the audience chamber; they were all hung with tapestries changed once a week. His sideboard of plate is worth 25,000 ducats, his silver is estimated at 150,000 ducats, while in his own chamber are always vessels worth 30,000 ducats.[1]

Such an imbalance of power was never going to last, and the king summarily swept the lofty cardinal from office in 1529 for his failure to procure papal approval for Henry's divorce from Catherine of Aragon. He confiscated York Place to use as his and Anne Boleyn's palace, choosing to overlook that it belonged to the northern archdiocese and not to Wolsey personally.

Between 1529 and 1533, Henry also compulsorily purchased all the St James's land to the west of King Street, encircling it with a ten-feet-high brick wall. The chronicler Edward Hall describes the purchase:

the Kyng had purchased the Bysshop of Yorkes place, which was a fayre Bysshops house, but not meete for a Kyng: wherefore the Kyng purchased all the medowes about saynt James, and all the whole house of S.James and ther made a fayre mansion and a parke, & builded many costly and commodious houses for great pleasure.[2]

The Horse Guards site already had buildings on it when purchased by King Henry. At the southern end of the site, on a point covered today by Dover House, stood the Bell inn. A little to its north, a well-worn lane ran up from the St James's scrubland where farm animals were grazed, across what is now Horse Guards Parade, to pass the Bell and join King Street. This junction locality was known colloquially as 'The Green'; at one time a stone cross, perhaps marking a parish boundary, also stood nearby on an area of residual grassland, 50 yards south of where the parish boundary is now marked on the underside of Horse Guards arch. A willow marsh called Steynour's Croft, where osiers for wickerwork were farmed, then covered much of the area we know today as Horse Guards Parade. Straggling north from the area of 'The Green', property developer John Millyng had erected, by the late 1400s, seven houses and a barn along the west of the highway. Some of these first recorded occupants of the Horse Guards site pause in their day's work to look back at us over the centuries – John Broke, clerk of chancery; John James, cellarer to the abbey, who also ran two shops in Tothill Street, a farm in Hampstead, and three wives; Henry Marbull, Westminster chief constable; and Thomas Maysent, fruit and vegetable wholesaler to Tothill Street market in Westminster. As the century turned, the properties on Horse Guards' site expanded into more tenements, housing artisans and officials who found a living in the archbishop's big house over the road, or at the Westminster abbey and palace complex ten minutes' walk down King Street. By the 1520s, however, most of the tenements covering Horse Guards' site had been replaced by the large mansion of Dr Richard

11

Duck, Dean of the York Place chapel in Cardinal Wolsey's time.[3]

After demolishing all the properties that had occupied the future Horse Guards site, Henry set out his palace tiltyard there, between the new park wall and King Street. In origin, a tiltyard was an enclosed arena where armoured knights fought each other in contest to simulate battle encounters. For the duration of Henry's palace rebuilding works (about five years), the north of the Tiltyard, formerly Dr Duck's property, was used as the main palace joinery yard. The location was to retain its identity – 'The Woodyard' – until Georgian times.

Although no official document exists confirming it, from about this date York Place assumed a new identity as 'Whitehall', probably deriving from the large areas of new white decoration called 'antik work' that appeared on many wall surfaces of the remodelled palace. It is likely, too, that the king acquiesced to the wishes of Anne Boleyn, who had a known fondness for this decorative style. William Shakespeare clearly marks the change of the palace's identity in his play *Henry VIII*, IV.i:

> Sir, you must no more call it York Place; that's past:
> For since the Cardinal fell, that title's lost;
> 'Tis now the King's and called Whitehall.

The new palace of Whitehall was largely complete by 1534, though additions continued to 1536. Its basic topography was to be a decisive factor in the origin of the military guard that was to culminate in the establishment of the Horse Guards building. In brief, its layout was achieved as follows.

Dominating the whole structure was the vast Privy Gallery block. It was transported, in pieces, from Wolsey's confiscated Waynflete Palace at Esher, to be reconstructed in 'the medowe directelye ayenst the saide manor [of] late Doctor Dookys [Duck's]'; also sent were 'bourde, lathe and playstre'.[4] This re-erected gallery ran east to west from the Thames to the highway that it joined at a point just south of today's Banqueting House. It continued across King Street at first-floor level through the newly built Holbein Gate – an octagonal-towered brick construction that stood across the street, next to the site of the present Dover House. From this gate, the gallery carried on west over the Dover House site to enclose the south end of the palace Tiltyard as the first-floor Tiltyard Gallery. At the park end of the Tiltyard Gallery, a private flight of stairs led down into the new St James's Park. The York Place main gate was retained, but renamed as the Court Gate, and stood on the point where Horse Guards Avenue now joins Whitehall. Also, as in York Place times, the new Court Gate continued to incorporate the public lane down to the ferry landing stage, the latter becoming known henceforth as Whitehall Stairs. Even Henry VIII could not usurp the ancient public rights of way on King Street and the ferry lane; the Holbein Gate allowed public traffic back and forth through its base, and courtiers passed between palace and park through its upper levels. Incidentally, Hans Holbein never designed the gate given his name, though he may have used its upper rooms as a studio on occasion, nor was this gate ever an official entrance to the palace; its only purpose was to span the public highway. It looked virtually identical to the surviving Tudor entrance gate to St James's Palace today.

The envisaged interior of Whitehall Palace. In rooms and galleries identical to these the officers of the Stuart Household regiments conducted their duties in protection of the monarch. These illustrations are early 20th-century watercolour representations of the interior of Knole House at Sevenoaks, Kent, where probably the most comprehensive collection of Stuart furniture and furnishings in the country is housed. As many of the items illustrated were originally at Whitehall Palace and in fact are still at Knole today, so the representation can be said to closely depict how the state rooms of Whitehall looked in Restoration times. (Author's collection)

All the principal Whitehall staterooms led off the Privy Gallery, the windows of which, to its south, looked out over one of the earliest of English formal gardens, the Privy Garden. The private royal apartments faced out across the Thames side of the palace and backed on to the other great palace artery, the Matted Gallery, with its ceiling by Holbein, which ran north to south at first-floor level. Below it, at ground-floor level, ran the Stone Gallery, bordering the east side of the Privy Garden as a kind of cloistered walk or loggia. Where, at first-floor level, the Matted Gallery and the Privy Gallery met at right angles were sited the King's extensive suite of private ('Privy') apartments. The whole palace was protected from flood by Henry's construction of the earliest stone Thames embankment. Stretching 700 feet in length, it was pierced in its centre by the Privy Stairs, the royal watergate. The remains of Henry VIII's embankment today lie under the east wall of the Ministry of Defence. To the north of the Court Gate, the Scotland Yard locality housed all the palace service quarters: the butteries, kitchens, stores, stables, etc. At its greatest extent, Whitehall Palace would sprawl across 23 acres.

Henry's Whitehall Tiltyard occupied the Horse Guards site longitudinally to the west of King Street. This specific location was chosen because it was highest above river level so less liable to degenerate into mire under the hooves of many galloping horses. From the Tiltyard the ground sloped down to St James's in the west, and to the Thames in the east.

The dimensions of the Whitehall Tiltyard were about 160 yards in length and 30 yards in width: today about the distance from Dover House to the wall of old Admiralty House. Running down the centre of the yard for about one-third of its length was the 'tilt', a fence-like construction of boards, some 5 feet high, which served to divide the approach paths of the galloping knights, so preventing head-on collisions. This had originally been canvas, or 'teld', from its Continental origins. Across the south end of the Tiltyard still ran the public path giving access to St James's, though now it was gated with a palace gatekeeper to determine who should pass. Adjoining the pedestrian gate was a larger

Whitehall in 1529. To relate the plan to modern Whitehall, the Banqueting House today stands to the left of the words 'York Place'. The Tiltyard (and later Horse Guards) would be built largely on the site of the Bell inn opposite and the adjoining site marked 'Duck'. The latter was the residence of Dr Richard Duck, Dean of Wolsey's chapel. The transformation of Wolsey's York Place into Whitehall Palace was commenced by Henry VIII after Wolsey's fall in October 1529.

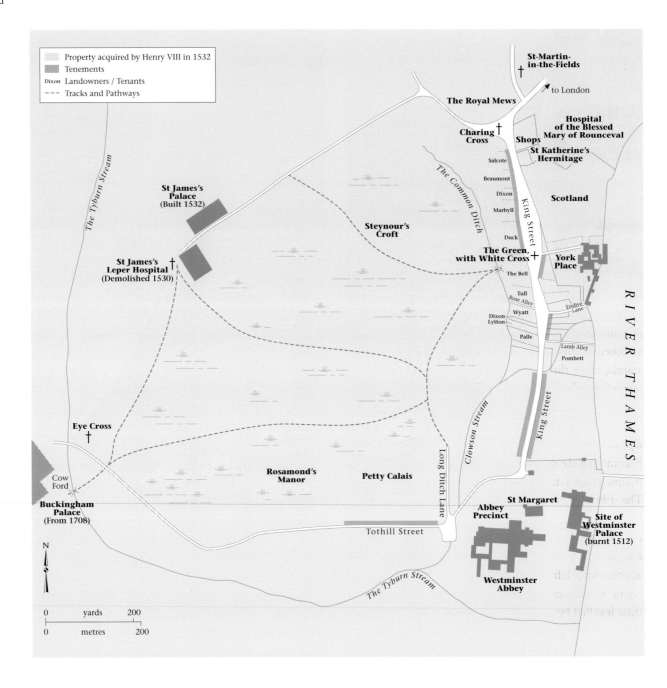

Legend:

- ☐ Property acquired by Henry VIII in 1532
- ▦ Tenements
- Dixon Landowners / Tenants
- - - - Tracks and Pathways

St-Martin-in-the-Fields †

to London

The Royal Mews

Hospital of the Blessed Mary of Rounceval

Charing † Cross

Shops

St Katherine's Hermitage

Salcote

Beaumont

Scotland

Dixon

Marbyll

King Street

The Common Ditch

St James's Palace (Built 1532)

Steynour's Croft

Duck

The Green, with White Cross †

York Place

St James's Leper Hospital (Demolished 1530) †

The Bell

Tull

Rose Alley

Endive Lane

Wyatt

Dixon Lytton

Palle

Lamb Alley

Pomhett

R I V E R   T H A M E S

The Tyburn Stream

Clowson Stream

King Street

Eye Cross †

Cow Ford

Buckingham Palace (From 1708)

Rosamond's Manor

Petty Calais

Long Ditch Lane

Tothill Street

Abbey Precinct

St Margaret

Site of Westminster Palace (burnt 1512)

Westminster Abbey

The Tyburn Stream

N

0   yards   200
0   metres   200

one allowing access for mounted horsemen. The public watched events in the Tiltyard from specially erected stands, while the royal family and courtiers viewed the scene from the Tiltyard Gallery to the south.

TOURNAMENTS AT WHITEHALL

By the time of Whitehall, tiltyard contests had become purely sporting occasions with a complicated points system to determine the 'Champion at Tilt'. The tiltyard event was named a tournament, and it comprised variations on three basic methods of combat. The first was the Joust, where opposing knights rode towards each other at a fast canter, approaching left hand to left hand across the tilt, and trying to unhorse each other with a direct blow from their levelled lances. Hits (*attaints*) were awarded on a scale according to the difficulty of the hit obtained. Striking an opponent's horse invoked penalties.

Second was the Tourney, consisting of knights, mounted or not, fighting hand-to-hand with swords, maces or halberds. A variation was the Baston course, whereby the contestants attempted to knock the crests off each other's helmets, the loser being 'crestfallen'.

The final method of combat was Barriers, where the knights fought on foot across the tilt using spears, maces, hand-axes or two-handed swords in a test of parrying skill. In later times this developed into a mock assault on a fanciful castle.

In contrast to popular belief, tournament armour was not that irksome to wear, the weight being distributed over all the body. Indeed a modern Household Cavalryman, to pass his training, has to mount his horse from the ground unaided, in full cuirasses and uniform.[5]

Any combatant knight required a string of appropriately trained horses known as 'destriers'.

A typical tournament armour of c.1515. The attached 'target' was an aiming point for the opponent's lance and also served to prevent the extremely costly armour from acquiring impact dents which (just like a modern car) were very expensive to repair. Note too the supporting bracket designed to take much of the weight of the lance. The joust led to saddles having a more upright cantle (back) and to lances being hollowed for some of their length to allow easy splintering on partial impact. The Duke of Suffolk's lance in the Tower of London is typical at 14$\frac{1}{2}$ft long, 20lbs in weight, and 27in. round its thickest part. (reproduced by permission of the Trustees of the Wallace Collection, London)

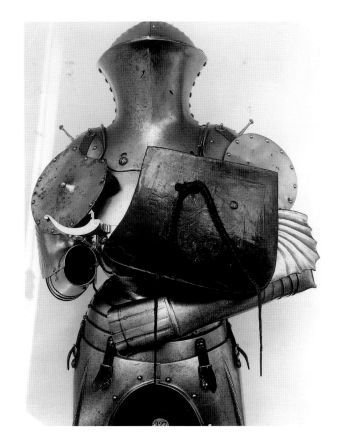

Deriving from the Latin *dextra*, meaning 'right-handed', these mounts were schooled to canter with right foreleg leading, the resultant gait slanting the horse's body slightly during its forward momentum so allowing the rider's lance to be squarely presented to the opponent. Henry VIII's 30 or so tournament horses were trained by Sir John Gostwick at his Willington estate in Bedfordshire where traces of the practice tiltyard can still be seen. Tournament horses were armoured around the head and neck, and the brass headpiece worn at the top of a Household

Cavalry horse's harness remains as a relic of the 'crinet' of protective armour that once covered it from ears to saddle. The type of horse used was not the 'cart horse' breed, but more the heavy hunter, very like the modern Household Cavalry horses.

Preliminary to a tournament, the knights would set up their pavilions, some in the Whitehall Tiltyard itself, at its north end, and some outside in St James's, where notices of the types of combat offered were often nailed to a tree. (Horse Guards Parade remained lined around with trees well into Victoria's reign.) A typical 'challenge' notice might depict variously coloured shields with the following explanations:

The first shield White, signifying to the Jousts; whoso toucheth that to be answered five courses.
The second Red, signifying to the Tourney; whoso toucheth that to be answered twelve strokes with the Sword, edge and point rebated.
The third Yellow, signifying to the Barriers, whoso toucheth that to be answered at the Barriers twelve strokes with a one-handed sword, the point and edge rebated.
The fourth Blue, signifying to the Assault, and whoso toucheth that to assault the said Castle with sword and target and morice pike with edge and point rebated.[6]

The knights chose their contest type from these notices, and so became the 'answerers' responding to the 'challengers' who put up the notices. Organizing it all were the heralds, who scrutinized coats of arms as valid and thus weeded out gatecrashers and 'batons of bastardy' alike. Points in a contest were awarded for, or against, contestants on a form called a 'cheque'.

Many of these survive today and most adhere to the following rules:

Breaking a spear from a hit ('attaint') between waist and neck:	1 point
Breaking a spear from a hit above the neck:	2 points
Breaking a spear from a hit and unhorsing opponent:	3 points
Breaking a spear from a hit on a saddle:	forfeit 1 point
Striking the Tilt once with a spear:	forfeit 2 points
Striking the Tilt twice with a spear:	forfeit 3 points
Striking the Tilt thrice with a spear:	forfeit all prizes
Losing helmet:	forfeit all prizes

Many additional variations of these rules existed for Tourney and Barriers contests.[7]

Tournament participation was only for the monied elite, as preparation and presentation costs could be astronomical. This brief bill for the Duke of Rutland's appearance in the Whitehall Tiltyard lists just a portion of the costs he incurred; it also shows he paraded in a chariot with a trumpeter before the main event:[8]

Paid the armorer for worke and servis at my Lorde's tyltinge	£2-13-6
Paid the painter for worke about the same businesse	£2-10-0
Paid for my Lorde's tilting stafes then used	£1-9-0
Paid for my Lorde's part of the trumpeter's apparrell, and chariot at the tylting,	£15-0-0
to Laborne, sadler,	£18-13-4
to Fisshe, the bittmaker,	£1-7-0
to Carter, the hatter	£12-0-0
to South, cuttler,	£2-11-6

Putting these expenses into context, a Tudor labourer might earn 4d a day in a good week; a skilled builder, perhaps 8d. Over a year the latter might bring home £10. To feed a family on just barley (the cheapest grain) for a year would cost about £3.

The tournament opened with a parade by the knights, at which they displayed dress shields of papier-mâché with exotic allegorical designs. These *impresa*, as they were known, were then handed to the spectating royalty to be hung on the walls of the royal reception gallery over the Privy Stairs watergate. As a result, this gallery was known as the Shield Gallery.

Original jousting scoring 'cheques'. Dating from c.1570 and showing how the tournament heralds tallied the points scored against each participant knight's coat of arms. The different symbols show where spears have been broken, penalties and the number of courses run. (Bodleian Library, University of Oxford, Ashmole 845)

This Tudor illustration encapsulates the vital components of Tiltyard tournaments. The fully armoured knights splinter lances at the gallop; the contestant at right has received a near fatal blow, forcing open his helmet visor. The boarded tilt is shown, as are the temporary stands for the spectators. The heralds appear in numbers, ensuring the correct running of the tournament, including the final prize-giving to the 'Champion at Tilt' by the royal personage. A more detailed view of a Whitehall tournament exists in an untraceable document of the Wood-Acton family. (British Library, Cott.Jul.E. IV, 6, f.15v)

OPPOSITE
George Clifford, Earl of Cumberland, Champion at Tilt, c.1590. He is dressed in typically extravagant finery ready for an Elizabethan tournament. His impresa shield is shown at top right. His armour, etched and tooled in gold intaglio fashion, would have cost a fortune. With all participants attired in like manner, the Horse Guards Tiltyard was resplendent during tournaments. (Topfoto)

With its walls covered from floor to ceiling with impresa from scores of Tudor and Jacobean Whitehall tournaments, the gallery must have looked breathtakingly beautiful when sunlight sparkling off the Thames shone through its windows to illuminate its heraldic splendour. The diarist John Manningham listed many of the impresa designs he saw during a visit there in 1601.[9] The Shield Gallery's colourful magnificence continued to make it a popular palace venue for meeting and greeting well into the time of that other great diarist, Samuel Pepys.[10]

The Horse Guards Tiltyard was to be the scene for all the above-described spectacles, and many others. What appears to be the earliest royal Tiltyard occasion occurred on 30 May 1533 to celebrate Anne Boleyn's coronation; however, as Windsor Herald Charles Wriothesely records, it may have been something of a non-event: 'the Mayor and his brethren had a goodly standing but there were few spears broken as the horses would not couple'.[11] A few weeks later, Anne delivered a baby girl, the future Queen Elizabeth, and celebrations were even more muted: the birth confounded the forecast of 'physicians, astrologers, wizards and witches whom affirmed it would be a boy', as recorded by Hapsburg ambassador Eustace Chapuys.[12]

The king himself competed little from the mid-1530s, after falling from his horse and suffering armour lacerations to his leg. At Whitehall, he contented himself watching events from the Tiltyard Gallery, often in an improvised wheelchair, his 'tramm', several of which were secreted along the Privy Gallery. Certainly the high point of Henry's Tiltyard endeavours was in May 1540, when, in response to the Pope's threat to collude in an invasion of England, he ordered a tournament challenge to be 'Proclaymed in France, Flanders, Scotland and Spain for all comers that will come against the chalenges of England'. The challenge comprised 14 separate contest types and was to be spread over a year and a day. According to Wriothesely, it succeeded all expectations: 'no person was denied to come in of any honestie, and their had meate and drincke at any tyme when they would aske itt...'[13] It had been one of Henry's finest hours.

Seven years later, on 28 January 1547, Henry died. This recalcitrant, fractious monarch played a key role in the history of Horse Guards: in Whitehall, he had given his country a sole focus of national authority, literally and nominally, that would last to the present day.

Tudor pageants of chivalry

Henry's successor, the physically weak but bright Edward VI (r.1547–53), took virtually no part in Tiltyard activities; barely a dozen entries exist in the official records for the whole of his reign describing any Tiltyard events at any of his palaces. Apart from Whitehall, each of the other principal Tudor palaces – Greenwich, Hampton Court and Richmond – had its own tiltyard. At Whitehall he is recorded as participating once or twice in *Juego des canas*, a Spanish variant of the joust using canes instead of lances.[14] Regrettably, his performances did not merit worthy contemporary comment.

Edward's successor, the Roman Catholic Mary Tudor (r.1553–58), used the Tiltyard even less: festive events were few and far between in her reign. More typical is her use of it as an *al fresco* court of law. Following the siege of Whitehall by James Wyatt's rebels in 1553, some survivors of the subsequent purge were brought to the Tiltyard the following February. Undertaker by profession and diarist by inclination, Henry Machyn had come to Whitehall with an eye to business, but then, as he recorded, 'all the Kent men bound with cords two and two together, went through London to Westminster. At the Tilt the poor persons kneeld down in the mire and there the Quen's grace looked out from the Gate and gave them all pardon,

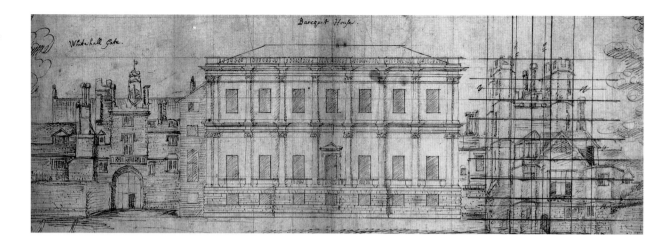

Whitehall Palace viewed from within the Tiltyard in 1623. This view is from a stage scenery plan by Inigo Jones for a Jacobean masque performed in 1623. Seen opposite is Jones's masterpiece, the Banqueting House, externally completed in 1622. To the left is the Court Gate, the main formal entrance to Whitehall Palace. It was the location of the Court Gate that determined the siting of the first Horse Guards building directly opposite so as to provide maximum security. The Court Gate stood where Horse Guards Avenue now joins Whitehall. At the extreme right of this view can be seen the windows of the Tiltyard Gallery: the Court's viewing point; behind and towering over all, looms the Holbein Gate. This was the view enjoyed by the Old Horse Guards' sentries throughout the Stuart era. (Inigo Jones, Conway Library, Courtauld Institute of Art, London)

and they cried out God save Queen Mary.'[15] The 'Gate' would have been the top floor of the Court Gate, which overlooked the Tiltyard from across the road.

It is with the reign of Elizabeth I (r.1558–1603) that Tiltyard events become their most plentiful and diverse. Animal baiting sports occurred in the Tiltyard now more often than tournaments, the latter often reserved as state occasions to impress influential foreign dignitaries. The royal court would watch animal baiting events from the Tiltyard Gallery with the windows closed – to avoid being spattered by the bloody entrails of disembowelled baiting hounds. Various descriptions of the gallery exist, including Von Wedel's account of 1584:

we got into a passage right across the Tiltyard; the ceiling is gilt, and the floor ornamented with mats. There were fine paintings on the walls, among them the portrait of Edward, the present Queen's brother...[16]

Gilbert Talbot, a courtier in 1578, remembered the Tiltyard Gallery somewhat differently:

I happened to walk in the Tiltyard under the gallery where her Majesty used to stand to see the running at Tilt, where by chance she was, and looking out of the window, my eye was fall towards her; she shewed to be greatly ashamed thereof, for that she was unready, and in her night stuff; so when she saw me at after dinner she gave me a great fillip on the forehead.[17]

The following two accounts give a hint of the colourful nature of Tiltyard contests where contestants had to look their best as well as compete their best in front of the monarch. Henry Machyn describes a 1559 Tiltyard contest:

There were gret justes at the quens pallas, and ther was my Lord Robert Dudley and my Lord of Hunsdon the chalengers, and they all wear in skarffes of whyt and blak, boyth the heraldes and trumpeters and deffenders with others in skarffes of red and yellow sarsenett...[18]

A decade or so later, George Delves wrote the following account to the Earl of Rutland:

Lord Oxford has performed his challenge at tilt, turn and barriers, far above the expectation of the world, and not much inferior to the other three challengers. The Earl's livery was crimson velvet, very costly. He himself and the [horse] furniture was in some more colours, yet he was the Red Knight. Charles Howard was the White Knight; Sir Henry Lee the Green Knight, Mr. Hatton was the Black Knight, whose horses were all trimmed with caparisons of black feathers.[19]

Sir Henry Lee, Master of the Armoury, and many times Champion at Tilt, was Elizabeth's principal tournament organizer. The greatest Elizabethan tournaments were staged annually for her accession and birthday anniversaries, 17 November and 7 September respectively, but any other distinctive social or national event requiring celebration could also result in a Tiltyard festival. Today the tradition continues with the annual staging of the Queen's Birthday Parade – 'Trooping the Colour' – in virtually the identical arena.[20]

The following list gives some idea of the diversity of the Horse Guards Tiltyard events in Elizabethan times: Tilt and Tourney of the Inner Temple (January 1562); Jousts, Tourney and Barriers to celebrate the wedding of Ambrose Dudley and Anne Russell (November 1565); Jousts and fight at barriers with swords on horseback to entertain the French Marriage Embassy (February 1579); Jousts to assail 'The Fortress of Perfect Beauty' for the French ambassadors (May 1581); Jousts between ten married men and ten bachelors (December 1584); Jousts to celebrate victory over the Spanish Armada (August 1588); The 'Two Thousand Feather Triumph' of Sir Walter Raleigh in praise of the Earl of Leicester's exploits in the Netherlands (June 1585); Barriers for Shrovetide (March 1595); and Barriers for Twelfth Night by the Middle Temple members (January 1598). These tournaments were so popular and well attended that during the 1581 event, some temporary stands in the Tiltyard collapsed under the weight of the spectators.[21] For the 1588 event, Elizabeth had carved a

Whitehall showing the Tiltyard wall to the right, c.1638. At the far end of the Tiltyard wall can be seen a small entrance for pedestrians with an adjoining larger entrance for horsemen and vehicles. The low roof visible to the right was where the tournament paraphernalia was once stored, scaffolding, planking for stands, and the like, though by this date it was more a wood and workmen's shed. The shrubs are evidence of the end of tournaments. Abutting the left side of the massive Holbein Gate is the west end of the Privy Gallery block. The Banqueting House dominates the left of the view, while to the right is Henry VIII's Great Close tennis court, fragments of which survive in the Treasury walls. (Guildhall Library, City of London)

Latin verse applauding the defeat of the Armada over the Tiltyard gate leading into the Park. A point of unusual interest in the 1579 event exists where some contestants are described as dressed like 'amazons, long hair hanging down their backs, wearing elaborate kirtles [short skirts] of rich material'.[22] Perhaps a Tudor precedent for participants in the beach volleyball contests planned to take place on Horse Guards Parade in the London 2012 Olympics?

In February 1601, an eclipse of entertainment occurred when the Earl of Essex attempted an armed coup to depose the queen. His naive plan to storm the Court Gate and overpower the Yeomen of the Guard in the palace galleries was quickly leaked to Elizabeth's intelligence service. Substantial numbers of the Trained Bands militia were brought into Whitehall from the Home Counties to maintain law and order as the conspirators were rounded up for summary treatment, the Court Gate itself being guarded by Rowland Lytton's 300 men from Hertfordshire. Providing a 24-hour infantry guard on the palace main gate, they are likely to have used the open area afforded by the south end of the Tiltyard as a secure assembly point for this duty; these men of the Hertfordshire Hundreds of Cashio and Dacorum were destined to make a return to Tiltyard duty to cope with the turmoil of a later reign.

On 24 March 1603, Elizabeth died; things were never to be the same again. Staged events at Whitehall under her successors were to follow a completely different thematic ideal, but in any case all conceptions of festivity were to be submerged under the tidal wave of civil war within a generation. The words of diarist Henry Goldwell from a few years earlier were more prophetic than he could have known: 'and thus ceased these courtlie triumphs, set foorth with most costlie braverie and gallantnesse'.[23]

The body of the queen was brought to Whitehall from Richmond. As Sir John Peyton informed Lord Salisbury, 'by 10 o'clock the King was proclaimed at Whitehall upon the Green, right against the Tiltyard'.[24] As mentioned earlier, 'The Green' was located near the south of the Tiltyard; however, by the 17th century, after years of building developments and increasing road traffic, it is doubtful that any actual 'green' remained. What is probably the last definite mention of 'The Green' as such occurs in 1515, during Cardinal Wolsey's time, when some York Place accounts mention 'a breke wall from the brode gate ayenst the Grene unto the grete gatehouse of my lords place'.[25] Nevertheless, that specific point of Whitehall was to retain its nominal identity up to 1698.

Proclamation locations are of the utmost regal significance, and 'The Green' area was so used from the reign of Edward VI (1547) to that of William and Mary (1689). This point was used because it faced the main gate leading to the Court; public notices of major importance – such as a copy Proclamation – pasted on the Court Gate would have been in full view of all visitors and passers by. Shakespeare, writing in 1613, confirms its continuing contemporary importance by having Sir Thomas Lovell reply to the question 'What news?' with, 'I hear of none but the new proclamation that's clapp'd upon the Court-gate' (*Henry VIII*, I.iii). After the later burning of the Court Gate in 1698, the Horse Guards building assumed the role of public news disseminator, with official public notices, including proclamations, being pasted on the outside of the sentry boxes up to the 1953 Coronation.

From masque to martyr

The dour King James I (r.1603–25) only spent the winter months and state occasions at Whitehall: he abhorred the necessity of living in London, 'that filthie toune'.[26] During his reign, Tiltyard activity was largely centred around the Accession Day Tilts (24 March), in which his dynamic son Henry, Prince of Wales, played a leading role. To develop his tournament technique, Henry built the first riding school of its kind at St James's Palace in 1607–09. In this school, he practised his equestrian skills on the many horses sent to him by the royal families of Europe.[27] But on the young prince's early death from typhoid in November 1612, events in the Tiltyard assumed a different character, the Jacobean masque taking centre stage. William Shakespeare, Ben Jonson, Inigo Jones and Richard Burbage all appear providing, respectively, mottoes, speeches, staging and themes for the participants.[28] But such was the complexity of the spectacles now attempted in the Tiltyard – including, in 1610, an elephant with a castle on its back – that the decision was taken to build a banqueting facility capacious enough to stage such productions.

Designed by Inigo Jones, completed in 1622 and still standing today, the Banqueting House provides, together with Horse Guards, the last visible link to the palace of Whitehall. In 1622, to keep passing traffic at

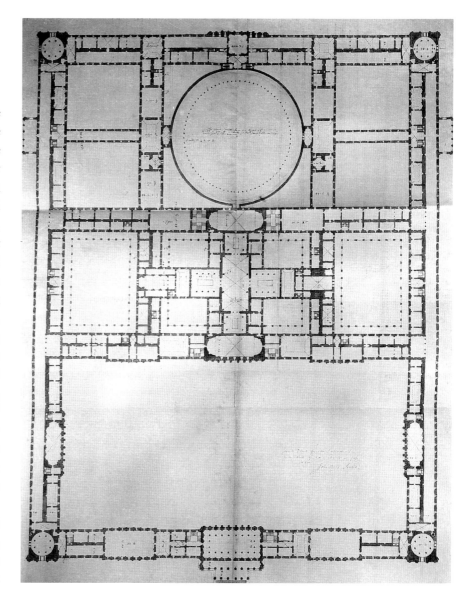

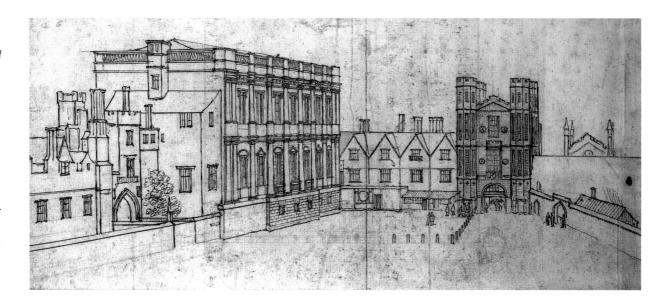

Whitehall, c.1640. A closer viewpoint showing further Tiltyard detail, namely the two access gates, which are at this date guarded by a park keeper in the low roofed building just visible – its chimney indicating a fireplace and sedentary occupation. Tournaments have long ceased by this time. The pre-1530 width of the highway in the foreground is magnified by the restricting arch under the Holbein Gate through which all traffic between Charing Cross and Westminster had to pass in both directions for two centuries. (Wenceslaus Hollar, Pepys Library, Magdalene College, Cambridge)

a safe distance and protect its coloured facade of Oxford stone on the first storey and Northampton stone above, 'xii great postes' were set up 'between the Court Gate and the raile next the Tiltyard wall'.[29] The 'raile' performed the same protective function for the stone Tiltyard wall that ran parallel to the highway. Sadly, the coloured stone façade of the Banqueting House was replaced in 1829 with the present monochrome Portland stone.

An interesting echo from this reign exists in the parish boundary marks depicted on the underside of Horse Guards arch: 'StMW/StMF'. These denote the parish of St Margaret's Westminster to the south and that of St Martin-in-the-Fields to the north. This line of parochial division is further marked above the east and west entrances to the archway by lead plaques. This boundary line dates from letters patent issued by James on 3 August 1604 during his improvements to the Park,

whereby he confined the franchise of Westminster Abbey to the south of a line defined as passing through the ornamental water in St James's Park. At this date, the 'ornamental water' comprised a residual loop of the nearby Tyburn stream, popularly called Rosamond's Pond. As well as this external definition of the boundary, it is also marked on Horse Guards' interior. Originally this demarcation took the form of a scrubbed white wood strip running east to west across the floors of both the central room above the arch facing the Parade, and the adjoining suite facing out to Whitehall. Over time this has given way to a black line above the door of the Major-General's office marked with 'SMW' to the south and 'SMF' to the north of the line, together with an adjoining explanatory brass plaque.

Despite passing an Act in 1603 'to restraine the inordinate hauntinge and tiplinge in Innes and Alehouses' – ostensibly to keep the London *hoi polloi* in order – James had a private drinking grotto built for himself and his cronies in the basement of the Banqueting House; it would not be long before the byword for the court became sleaze. Just one example will suffice to illustrate the questionable character of events that oftentimes spilled into the Horse Guards Tiltyard. At the state reception in 1606 for the visit of James's brother-in-law, King Christian IV of Denmark, various young women assumed allegorical roles in the service of the royal visitor, namely the Queen of Sheba and Faith, Hope and Charity. The first managed to dump her basin of sweets, jellies and cream into the king's lap; the second was found vomiting in a courtyard; the third was speechlessly drunk; and Charity was prostrate in another room, having told the king she had no presents for him, he had too many already anyway! Thus lived Jacobean Whitehall.[30]

Not surprisingly, it is with James's reign that the Accession Day Tiltyard tournaments cease altogether. The final one was recorded in 1624, but even this one was postponed and perhaps never staged. In fact, the spectacle of animal baiting occurred more often in the Tiltyard in these years than tilting or masques, so much so that the Tiltyard Gallery became known as the 'Bearstake Gallery'. Baiting sports continued in the Tiltyard until 1660. The era came to an end on 5 May 1625, when workmen erected stands in the Tiltyard for the public to watch 'the solemnity of the funeral of our late Sovereign King James'.[31]

CHARLES I – WHITEHALL'S SORROW

James's son Charles I (r.1625–49) acceded to the throne with ideas considerably in advance of his purse and station in life: he decided that Whitehall

The death warrant of Charles I; Cromwell's name is third from top, on the left. By October 1660, 28 of the surviving regicides had been either executed or imprisoned for life. Cromwell, Henry Ireton, and Colonel Thomas Pride had already died, but they were reburied under the Tyburn gallows. In January 1662, the Restoration spy, Sir George Downing rounded up another three in Holland. They died on the scaffold, he received a baronetcy. (Topfoto/ Woodmansterne)

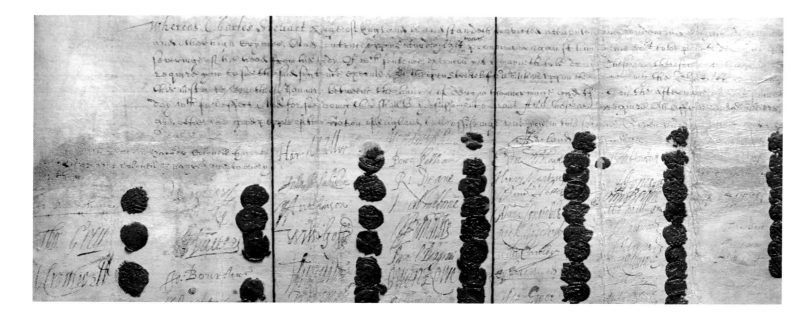

was not a good enough palace and asked Surveyor General Inigo Jones to prepare designs for a better one. Accordingly, Jones and his deputy, John Webb, produced a selection of plans for vast ranges of buildings that would have encompassed all of Whitehall and most of St James's Park as well. As conceived, the plans are a record of Jones's genius for Renaissance architectural composition. Had any of them been put into effect, England would have boasted the most prestigious palace then known, and Horse Guards probably would never have existed. But they were destined never to be more than a fantasy.[32]

Charles's days of building castles in the air were terminated by increasingly frequent confrontations with Parliament and population. Civil opposition to the king's 'holier than thou' doctrine manifested itself in secret meetings and street riots principally generated by and involving the militant apprentices. Proclamations were made 'to disperse loose persons gathered in a tumultuous manner'.[33] Nationwide the Trained Bands were raised to full alert. Tensions increased over the next decade and Rowland Lytton's old Hertfordshire unit sent to the deputy Lieutenants of Hertfordshire a 'Petition of the soldiers of the trained bands of the hundreds of Cashio and Dacorum':

> We humbly offer you these considerations, That from the bottom of our hearts we make profession of our faith and loyalty to the King and we shall be ready to spend our lives and dearest blood in defence of his person... That we have always been reputed to be the Kings Guards... That in 1601, when the Earl of Essex was beheaded, the trained bands of this county guarded the Court Gate at Whitehall by day and by night.[34]

This probably constitutes the earliest documented presence of a formal guard unit in the closest proximity to, if not within, the Horse Guards Tiltyard.

The precautions to maintain law and order within the precincts of both palace and Parliament were to prove inadequate. Consequently, on 28 December 1641, an entry in the Lord Chamberlain's accounts records 'A Warrant to Mr. Surveyor for ye building a Court of Guard before Whitehall'.[35] The speed with which this warrant was executed is evident in a letter to Sir Thomas Penington from Sidney Bere, dated 30 December 1641:

> Since the holidays there have been such rude assemblies and multitudes of the lesser sort of people, that every day threatened a desperate confusion, nor are we yet free from these fears. In fine, these distempers have so increased by such little skirmishes that now the train[ed] bands keep watch everywhere, all the courtiers are commanded to wear swords, and a corps-de-garde is built within the railes by Whitehall; all of which fills everyone with fears and apprehensions of greater evils.[36]

A 'corps-de-garde', or 'court of guard', was not so much a building in brick or stone for long-term domicile, but more a timber-built guardroom to house those Trained Band soldiers actually on duty 'within the railes', that is, in the south end of the Tiltyard. As such, it forms the earliest record of a standing guard on the Horse Guards site. The Tiltyard was chosen to site this security force because it controlled the main road to Parliament, it was directly opposite the main Court Gate, and there was space for a substantial number of soldiers to be assembled in safety behind its high retaining walls.

These points were tested within hours as Mr Dillingham wrote to Edward, Lord Montagu on 30 December 1641: 'The soldiers that watched at Whitehall Gate Tuesday night were not only warmed by a good fire without, but with a hogshead of wine within. You see we are beginning to please the people now. In the afternoon, the said soldiers issued out of Whitehall, and cut and hacked the apprentices that were passing to Westminster.'[37]

The king had vainly hoped that his military force would protect him from the consequences when, on 4 January 1642, he surrounded the House of Commons with 2,000 of his men and, forcing his way into the chamber, demanded that the members surrender to him the five who most vigorously opposed his demands. Parliament closed its ranks, played for time, and allowed the five members to slip away to safety. Publicly proven impotent against a united Parliament, Charles returned to Whitehall empty-handed; a week later, attended by those still loyal to him, he left for Oxford to set up his court there. He was to return to Whitehall again only for his death.

Civil war was imminent, and parliamentary forces took over the now virtually deserted palace. By the summer of 1642, all the approach roads to Whitehall and Westminster were barred with posts and chains, while around the perimeter of the capital was raised an earthwork barricade reinforced with a court-of-guard every few miles. The diary of a rural vicar, the Reverend Ralph Josselin, conveys a sense of the civil danger in these days. Having cause to visit London in August 1642, he deemed it expedient to 'provide for my self Sword, Halbert, Powder and Match'.[38]

The approach to Whitehall from Charing Cross was covered by a gun battery installed in the Prince Henry Wing, which formed the ground storey of the Privy Gallery abutting the Holbein Gate; the battery was to stay there for the next 80 years. Scots traveller William Lithgow describes the scene early in 1643: '...and what shall I say, I found the street-enravelled Court, before Whitehall Gate guarded also with a Court du Guard, a noveltie beyond novelties; and what was rarer, I found grasse growing deep in the royall Courts of the King's House which indeed was a lamentable sight.'[39] Lithgow, though florid in his description, clearly conveys the dereliction of Whitehall over which, nevertheless, a guard was maintained.

The expected threat to the capital did not materialize, for the king and his royalists were soundly beaten at Marston Moor in 1644 and at Naseby in 1645 by the Parliamentarian 'New Model' army commanded by Oliver Cromwell. An uneasy peace followed, and in July 1645 the defences of London were reduced, the House of Commons Journals recording that 'the Courts of Guard be forthwith pulled down and sold away'.[40] This possibly did not include the one inside the Tiltyard as later references will be seen to an 'old' guard quarters still *in situ* there.

Charles was not long licking his wounds before he made another attempt to impose his authority on the country, only to be decisively beaten again at Preston in August 1648. This time, Cromwell resolved to finish the issue once and for all: he marched his army to London, cleared Parliament of surviving opposition members and forced the remaining 'rump' to convene a court and try the now captive king for treason. The

This early 20th-century painting depicts the events of 30 January 1649. Cromwell's guards of Horse and Foot are seen parading from their Tiltyard and Whitehall quarters to control the crowds assembling outside the Banqueting House for the execution of Charles I. He was previously imprisoned in St James's Palace and had been escorted across the Park that morning by a guard of Ironsides. On the scaffold the Bishop of London is exchanging some last words with the tragic king. Today a plaque on the Banqueting House wall denotes the supposed window through which Charles stepped to his death. (Mary Evans Picture Library)

OPPOSITE

Oliver Cromwell. His army took over Whitehall Palace and his Life Guard was stationed in the Tiltyard during the Civil War. Bishop Burnet writes of the 'roughness of his education and temper', but Cromwell personally came to indulge at Whitehall all the Cavalier pleasures (later endemic there after the Restoration) that his regime sought to persecute and subdue. (Topfoto/ HIP/Royal Armouries)

outcome is history. On 30 January 1649, the King was escorted from St James's across the park, through the Tiltyard Gallery, to his execution outside the Banqueting House. Held back by the restraining arms of Cromwell's soldiers, the crowd watched; among the onlookers was a teenage Samuel Pepys (shown at left), scribbling notes on the scene that he would recall years later in his famous diary.[41]

The Ironsides guard Whitehall

The deserted apartments of Whitehall and St James's became a garrison as Cromwell's men moved in to control the government. The principal administrative offices for the military regime were ranged just south of the Tiltyard, near the Tudor Cockpit. Here were based the executive offices of the Board of Ordnance, the Treasurer at War, the Wagonmaster General, the Scoutmaster General (Intelligence branch), the Judge Marshal, the Military Secretary, the Physician, the Adjutant General, and the Quartermaster General and his commissary supply staff. Central control was exercised through a Council of War, which met several times a week in Cromwell's own office sited by the Cockpit, near present-day Downing Street. Responsible for communicating the Council's orders to the field units was the Military Secretary, a post held by William Clarke from 1656 to the Restoration. Palace security was also considered during these meetings:

> The Council has noticed several miscarriages committed by their guards arising from the absence of the Captain and officers, and that the Captain or next officers are to attend personally every day with the guard, and take care that no clamourous women nor spies be permitted to come within the walls of this house.[42]

A Tiltyard sutler's trade token. Issued by Edward Lloyd, 'Sutler to His Majesty's Guard of Foot'. The regimental description dates it to after the 1660 Restoration but before the first Horse Guards building of 1663–64. The stylized building shown, by law supposed to define the place of origin of the token, is definitely not Old Horse Guards but may represent Edward Carter's Tiltyard guardhouse of 1649. (© The British Museum)

The accommodation of Cromwell's Ironsides within the palace apartments was also causing problems. On 20 July 1649, the Council of State requested Sir Henry Mildmay 'to confer with the QMG as to how the soldiers in Whitehall may be quartered in Scotland Yard so that the rest of the house may be free'.[43] The agreed solution seems to have been to stable the mounted elements of the cavalry guard in Scotland Yard and allocate the Tiltyard to the foot soldiers. Some verification for this occurs when, on 20 October 1649, the Council of State issued a warrant to Edward Carter (Surveyor of Works), 'To build a Guard House in the Tiltyard near the wall of St. James's Park for better accommodation of the soldiers. Also to make up the gallery door next St. James's Park and set a lock to it.'[44] Presumably this new guardhouse was to be 'better

accommodation' compared to the original Court of Guard quarters of 1641. This is the first known record of a permanently accommodated guard on Horse Guards site, the need for it being the civil unrest following King Charles's execution. The 'gallery door' being closed off was the old park access from the Tiltyard Gallery.

A depiction of the first permanent guardhouse to occupy the Horse Guards site may exist, though there is not yet any confirmation of this. Edward Carter was deputy to Inigo Jones before being promoted to Surveyor of Works following Jones's disappearance in the Civil War. As shown by the buildings known to be by Carter, it is clear he tried to design his own versions of Jones's Renaissance architectural ideas. Housed in the British Museum collections is a trader's token that was in circulation at the Restoration and on which is depicted in stylized form a small two-storey building with distinctive features favoured by Carter: the high-hipped roof and minimalist classical decoration. The trader in question was a sutler in the Tiltyard: a provisions merchant supplying the military stationed there. These tokens circulated as monetary small change and were intended to unambiguously identify both the issuer and his place of work. This token (for $\frac{1}{2}$d) was issued by Edward Lloyd, and says he is, 'Suttler to His Maiesties Gard of Foot'. Around the time of the Restoration, this was undoubtedly correct regimentally, but one question remains: did his token also depict his place of work – Edward Carter's 1649 guardhouse of possibly classical design?[45]

The authority of the Parliamentarian army was countrywide, and in August 1650, before extending this authority into Scotland, the northern army commander, Sir Arthur Haselrigge, was ordered to raise a regiment of horse and two regiments of foot to police the border territory. Sir Arthur was one of the original 'five members' of the House of Commons sought by Charles I. His regiment of horse, as will be seen, still exists today as The Blues and Royals, while his foot soldiers became the Coldstream Guards, taking their name from the border village around which they were recruited. In June 1651, Haselrigge relinquished command of his mounted regiment to Colonel James Berry, and as the standard of the new colonel was blue in colour, so the wearing of the blue uniform by The Blues and Royals is said to have originated at this time.

One interesting sidelight on the military events of this time is the financing of Cromwell's army. This was achieved quite simply with the ransacking of the staterooms of Whitehall and sale of the valuables, often at a fraction of their true value. Charles had been the most prolific art collector in Europe, so paintings by Titian (his favourite artist – reputedly he had 21 Titians in his Privy apartments at Whitehall),[46] Correggio, Holbein, Tintoretto, Dürer and Rubens, for example, were listed at sale prices of £100 to £200 each, while Leonardo da Vinci's *St John* went for the absurdly low price of £140! In 1653, in a 'cash only, no questions asked' deal, the Council of State allowed the Spanish ambassador to export, duty free, 24 chests of such valuables. They went on 18 mules to Madrid. Most are still there, in the Prado; others grace the Louvre, the Koninklijk Museum voor Schone Kunsten, Antwerp, and the Kunsthistorisches Museum, Vienna, with just a few remaining in London's National Gallery.[47] In 1975, the Royal Academy managed to reassemble once more

in London many of these former Whitehall paintings in its exhibition 'The Golden Age of Spanish Painting'.

The heir to the throne, Prince Charles, had been crowned king by the Scots at Scone on 1 January 1651, and in an effort to usurp Cromwell's rule, he led an invading force into England later that year. But, like his father before him, he underestimated his opponent and the little army of Royalists was cut to pieces by Cromwell's Ironsides at Worcester in September 1651. The well-known sequel was the young king's six-week escape across country to France, including a day spent hiding in an oak tree. A close look at the state uniforms of the Horse Guards sentries will reveal the oak leaf and acorn motif commemorating this episode. Cromwell's commemoration of the battle was somewhat different: he ordered Colonel Berkstead 'to shoot the guns of his regiment and cause a bonfire to be made at Whitehall Gate in token of joy for the good news of the routing of the enemy near Worcester'.[48]

In 1653, Cromwell decided he ought to be seen to be the person of national authority that his assumption of the title Lord Protector of the Commonwealth implied. To this end, he refurbished the Banqueting House to properly receive foreign dignitaries and to conduct his version of state occasions. An early state visit was that, in March 1654, of the ambassadors of the States-General of Holland. But as a later Scandinavian observer recorded, the military that kept Cromwell in office was never far away and 'studded the wall on both sides' at the reception he attended.[49] But Cromwell did not stint himself. Not long after, in 1656, the diarist John Evelyn had a look around: 'I adventurd to go to White-Hall, where of

George Monck. The mastermind of the Restoration of Charles II, his military needs were a prime mover in the building of Old Horse Guards. Although astute enough to take charge of a country with no government or king in office, Monck found the subtleties of politics at the highest level beyond his abilities. Pepys was unimpressed and found him a 'dull, heavy man ... a Blocke-headed Duke I did never expect better from'. Monck commanded his own Troop of Horse Guards – 'His Grace the Duke of Albemarle's Troop of His Majesty's Life Guard' – from 1661 until his death in 1670. (Courtesy of Exeter City Council)

many yeares I had not ben, & found it very glorious & well furnish'd.'[50] The following year, no expense was spared for the Whitehall wedding of Cromwell's daughter Frances to Robert Rich. Said guest Sir William Dugdale, 'Forty eight violins and fifty trumpets were played and mixt dancing, hitherto considered profane, continued till 5 of the clock of the morning!'[51]

Even in exile Charles and his loyal courtiers were not safe, and in 1655 the self-styled Protector signed an alliance with France forcing the Royalists to flee to the Spanish Netherlands. Here, Charles negotiated with the king of Spain to organize his followers into a private army. On 2 April 1656, he was able to muster his own Life Guard commanded by Lord Gerard of Brandon; a regiment of English guards under Henry Wilmot, Earl of Rochester, who had masterminded the king's escape; a Scots regiment under the Earl of Middleton; and an Irish formation under the Duke of Ormonde. In 1657, another Scots regiment and two Irish were raised from escaping Royalist adherents. In April 1657, Charles's brother, James Duke of York, assumed overall command of this little army, having his own Life Guard commanded by Sir Charles Berkeley. Following various active service involvements, this embryo Royalist army was, by 1660, part of the Dunkirk garrison. Meanwhile, London was pitilessly repressed by the now Major-General Berkstead who banned any social event likely to conceal seditious intentions. As one newsletter records, 'The bears in the bear garden were killed, and the heads of the game cocks wrung off by a company of foot soldiers, also some hundred of women are committed to the Tower, not being able to give a satisfactory account of themselves.'[52] Actors, their playhouses dismantled, 'used to bribe the Officer who Commanded the Guard at Whitehall, and were therupon connived at to Act for a few Days, at the *Red Bull*; but they were sometimes notwithstanding Disturb'd by Soldiers'.[53]

Not surprisingly, an attempt was made to assassinate Cromwell by one Miles Sindercombe

in 1656. It only failed by chance, but as a result Cromwell moved his personal bodyguard into palace quarters at Whitehall. Thus, on 19 August 1656, Mr Embree (the new Surveyor of Works) ordered 'the building of a stable in the yard at Whitehall for use of His Highness's Life Guard'.[54] This was Cromwell's New Model Life Guard of Horse, which had recently increased in size and reorganized to eight squadrons of 20 men each. It was commanded by a Buckinghamshire gentleman, Major Beke (a son-in-law to Cromwell), as captain, with seven lieutenants, one cornet, one quartermaster and four trumpeters. In all probability, the 'yard' defined above was Scotland Yard: the Tiltyard, with several buildings in it for the Life Guard of Foot, could not have housed the extensive stabling facilities needed for a mounted force the size of the Life Guard of Horse. Interestingly, before long these same Cromwellian Scotland Yard stables were to house another significant force.

Oliver Cromwell died at Whitehall on 3 September 1658, and control of the country devolved upon his son Richard, who soon proved politically ineffective. The tide of sympathy for the exiled King and Court was swelling by the day and with fear of retribution now removed, all across the country in the village inns and town taverns, people were singing the following refrain by poet Martin Parker:

Though for a time we see Whitehall, with cobwebs hanging on the wall,
Instead of silk and silver brave, which formerly it used to have,
With rich perfume in every room, delightful to that Princely train:

A young Charles II, militarily attired in his cuirasses, c.1650s. By the time of his Restoration in 1660, the confident young man seen here had changed inexorably into a hollow-cheeked survivor, following the privations of his ten-year exile on the Continent. (Adrian Hannemann; this painting is in a private collection)

OPPOSITE
This anonymous ink depiction from an artist's 1720/30 sketchbook shows in some detail how the Whitehall backdrop looked from the Park. The sketch is obviously preparatory to a more finished work which, at present, remains unknown. The detailing of Horse Guards' cupola shows the encircling balcony, the single-handed clock, and the single bell hanging above. The balcony on the first floor level leads out from the central administrative office suites shared by the Secretary-at-War and the Guards commanders. (Author's collection)

Which again you shall see, when the time it shall be,
That the King enjoys his own again.[55]

The initiative to recall Charles from exile and re-establish the monarchy was taken by the astute commander of the Scottish Parliamentary army, General Monck. Following secret royalist meetings held at Nun Appleton, the secluded Yorkshire estate of the English army commander General Fairfax, the Restoration plans were drafted and communicated to the court in the Netherlands. Tacit approval was given, and with control of London the first essential step, Monck set off south on New Year's Day, 1660, escorted by Colonel Berry's Regiment of Horse and Haselrigge's Coldstream foot regiment, 'The Lord General's Regiment of Foot'. He arrived on 3 February having been applauded by an approving populace through every county en route. Pepys saw them arrive at Whitehall, 'in very good order with stout officers',[56] while another onlooker thought, 'The Foot had the best arms and were the likeliest men that I ever saw … all the officers had red and white favours in their hats, and the trumpeters and foot boys a red livery, laced with silver lace.'[57]

A month of political chess ensued until 16 March, when Monck arranged the dissolution of the old 'rump' parliament and the election of a new one to properly represent the population. That night London and Whitehall were lit up by street parties of rump-roasting bonfires! A fortnight later, Sir John Grenville and Lord Hyde, together with Charles, ratified the Declaration of Restoration at Breda. Charles had been at Brussels (then in Spanish hands), but Grenville met him secretly there and escorted him on a post-haste ride out of a country still at war with Britain. Breda was the first safe town they reached across the border. The document was returned to Westminster to be voted on by the newly elected assembly. Parliamentary approval of the Declaration followed on 1 May 1660, and the vote carried that Charles II be formally invited to return and assume his rightful place as head of state. But Monck had not achieved an unconditional victory: the price to be paid for the Restoration was the disbandment of the New Model Army, which for nearly two decades had imposed the will of the 'rump' parliament on an unwilling people.

While the paperwork for the reduction of the army was initiated, a civilian army was recruited and applied to the happier task of restoring Whitehall Palace to something like fit for a king. Valuables and furnishings that had been spirited away to safety before the rapacious Parliamentary regime could sell them were re-installed in the state-rooms, gardens replanted, lawns turfed and trimmed, galleries repaired and regilded, pictures rehung, roads and courtyards swept and repaved anew.[58] These efforts received a temporary set-back when a high spring tide flooded part of the palace, enabling Pepys to watch events 'from a boat rowed in King Street.'[59] But all was soon in order again, and on the site of the old Tiltyard 'Green', on 8 May 1660, Charles was officially proclaimed as King of England. Across the Channel, on 22 May, the royal party boarded the *Naseby* (later the *Royal Charles*) sent to bring them home; it set sail that night for Dover.

Old Horse Guards

Horse Guards from Restoration to Revolution

On 25 May 1660, the Restoration became fact when Charles II landed at Dover to be greeted by General Monck. He was escorted to London by his Life Guard, now numbering some 600, and comprising three troops, commanded by Lord Gerard of Brandon, Sir Charles Berkeley and Sir Philip Howard.

Back in Whitehall, the political clean-up operation continued with any residual dissident factions being rounded up. In a letter dated 23 July 1660, Venetian legate Francisco Giavanina noted, 'to protect the Court they have increased the guards at Whitehall – besides double sentries on foot they have added two on horse at every approach'.[60] Here is the first record of double mounted sentries keeping guard in Whitehall.

The Parliamentary army disbandment proceeded apace, and by mid-November 1660 only eight regiments remained; however, the garrison at Dunkirk was excluded from the Disbandment Act with the consequence that many 'retired' soldiers found their way there. Charles managed to save his own force of Life Guards by sending them there immediately after the Restoration had been effected; they were incorporated into the 'Duke of York's Life Guard of Horse'. Other Royalist followers at the garrison were

Charles II walking with his courtiers in St James's Park, c.1674. Charles enjoyed the amenity of St James's Park probably more than any other monarch, and al fresco Cabinet meetings became regular outings for his court. Behind the royal coach other courtiers are seen descending from the Tiltyard Gallery which formed the Park exit of the main Privy Gallery. The Tiltyard Guard is formed from the 2nd Foot Guards (Coldstream Guards); their sentry stands outside their guardroom. The park is seen teeming with animal life. This early view of Old Horse Guards shows the royal coat of arms in the pediment and the clock tower with east/west faces, both features carried over to the present building. Next to the Ensign holding the Colour is the post used at Guard Mounting for 'Lodging the Colour': possibly it was not permanent, but fixed in place for each parade. (Hendrick Dankerts, Topfoto)

*OPPOSITE
A 19th-century romantic view of a Restoration Household Cavalryman bowing to his king. (C. Clark, author's collection)*

enlisted into a foot guards regiment commanded by Lord Wentworth. As a gesture to Monck for his initiative in planning the Restoration (he had already created him Knight of the Garter and Duke of Albemarle), Charles replaced his Life Guard escort with the old 'Regiment of Horse' originally raised in the north, renaming it for its new role, 'The Royal Regiment'. Colonel Berry, its old commander, was replaced by Unton Crook, with Daniel O'Neale as his commanding officer, a veteran Royalist who had fought at Worcester. However, a now militarily wary Parliament was unmoved by the King's patronage of the 'Royal Regiment', and it too was ordered to disband by December 1660. In fact, by Christmas that year the only Cromwellian-era units that remained were the two raised at Coldstream by Haselrigge in 1650 – 'The Royal Regiment' and the 'Lord General's Regiment of Foot'.

THE BIRTH OF THE BRITISH ARMY

In 1660, there were several serious attempts to destabilize the new monarchy, and although the Parliamentary army units had to go as a condition of his return, Charles insisted to an extremely dubious Parliament that the monarchy would only last as long as his personal safety was assured. Reluctantly, the government assented to the raising of a small protective force designed solely to protect the court, so an establishment for 'Guards and Garrisons' was agreed. Charles's foresight in creating this force was vindicated within days. In his diary on 7 and 9 January 1661, Pepys wrote, 'This morning news was brought to me that there had been a great stir in the City this night by the Fanatiques who had been up and killed six or seven men ... two mornings later came a fresh alarm, so I arose and went forth.'[61]

Pepys was recording the final stand of a band of rioters called Fifth Monarchists whose aim was to overthrow King Charles and replace him with 'King' Jesus. The leader of the sect was a half-witted cooper, Thomas Venner, who with his followers, had now been chased to north London by the mounted troops of 'The Royal Regiment' and the infantry of Monck's Foot Guard. Although both faced imminent disbandment, they were the only military force immediately available to cope with the threat. The so-called Venner Riot concluded with a shoot-out over two days at the Blue Anchor tavern in Cripplegate, the Parliamentary units successfully snuffing out the danger to the king.

Charles, meanwhile, had been visiting the fleet at Portsmouth and on arrival back at Whitehall sat down with his Cabinet to make some far-reaching military decisions. He rescinded disbandment orders for the two units that had suppressed the riot, and also put into effect the raising of his own personal force – three troops of Cavalry and four regiments of Foot, the 'Guards and Garrisons' already approved by Parliament. On 26 January 1661, he signed its Royal Warrant and in so doing gave birth to the British Army of today.

But the old Cromwellian units had to be seen to disband. So on 14 February 1661, the duty contingent of Monck's regiment of foot left its Tiltyard quarters to march to Tower Hill and join the remainder of the regiment to formally lay down their arms in front of the four appointed Commissioners for Disbanding; they then took them up again in the king's service as the Lord General's Regiment of Foot Guards.[62] Two days later, the 'Royal Regiment' rode out of its Scotland Yard quarters to Tothill Fields in Westminster. The soldiers returned later that day still wearing their Cromwellian blue tunics and still designated as the 'Royal Regiment of Horse', but now officially in the service of the king.

This military manoeuvring by King and Parliament resulted in the creation of the following regiments, which still survive today and which were all to be centred at the Horse Guards building for their original administrative and duty roles:

'His Majesties own Troop of Guards'
'His Highness Royall the Duke of Yorke his Troop of Guards'
'His Grace the Duke of Albemarle his Troop of Guards'
– all today The Life Guards
'The Royal Regiment of Horse'
– today The Blues and Royals
'The King's Royal Regiment of Foot Guards'
– today the Grenadier Guards
'The Lord General's Regiment of Foot Guards'
– today the Coldstream Guards

On 2 April 1661, a further Scots Life Guard Troop, 'His Majesty's Troop of Guards', was raised in Edinburgh, this unit is also represented today by The Life Guards. A Scots Foot Guards regiment was also raised – today the Scots Guards.

To complete his embryo standing army, Charles was also allowed to use the Foot Guard unit still at Dunkirk under Lord Wentworth. On return to England, these soldiers, 'Wentworth's Foot Guards', were granted equal seniority with 'The King's Royal Regiment of Foot Guards'. When Wentworth died in 1665, these two regiments amalgamated to form 'The

Royal Regiment of Foot Guards', today the Grenadier Guards, as shown above.

QUARTERING THE GUARDS

By the late summer of 1661, concern had been raised about how to house these new royal regiments, barracks as such did not exist. Two entries from the Office of Works accounts show how the problem was initially addressed:

August 1661: Carpenters ... setting up of beds contayning fifty foote in length at the new guards house in the Tiltyard, Joysting and bourding the Flores in the old and new guard houses there contayning two squares and lxxxviii [88] foote.
Cleansing part of the great shore leading from the streete before Scotland Yard gate to the said docks (Scotland Docke) ... helping to dig up manger posts and other posts belonging to the stable which was pulled down in the outward court.[63]

This entry clearly defines the existence of two guardhouses in the Tiltyard: Carter's from 1649 was possibly one, the other perhaps the old Court of Guard. Both would have been subject to periodic renovations by surveyor John Embree. Stabling revision works to Cromwell's old Life Guard quarters in Scotland Yard are indicated where 'the great shore' means the main driveway access connecting the north of the palace complex to the highway: it exists today as Great Scotland Yard. The second entry details the substantial rebuild of the Foot Guard Tiltyard guard quarters:

September 1661: Warrant to pay Hugh May (Paymaster of Works) £500 on account, for repairs at Hampton Court for the King's speedy remove, and for building a guard for the foot soldiers in the Tiltyard.
... Carpenters ... takeing off the old bourdes and new bourding the roofe of the old guardhouse in the Tiltyard ... mending and making good the bourded roof of the other guard house there where the new chimney was ... setting making and fitting of two mantle trees and tassels for the two new chimney in the said guard houses ... making a ptition [partition] quartered and bourded in an upper roome there with a dore in it and enclosing the top of the staires there with quarters and slitt deals and a dore in it... Takeing downe a window and putting it up agayne in another place there ... making a cubbard there also for the officers to keepe their bookes in ... setting up a penthouse there and driving iron hookes for the souldiers to lay theire pikes on ... making and setting up two penthouses for the Horse Guard at Scotland Yard Gate... Bricklayers ... making a new chimney tenn foote wide and xvij [17] ffote high at the old Guard House in the Tiltyard and making another chimney in the new guard howse there vj [6] foote and a halfe wide and xvij [17] foote high.[64]

These renovations addressed the need for the centralized administration of the new Household troops. The comments 'upper roome' and 'staires' show a double-storied building, while 'a cubbard for the officers to keepe their bookes in' indicates a first focus of regimental command on the Horse Guards site for the two new Foot Guards regiments. The Household Cavalry stood guard at the 'two penthouses for the Horse Guard at Scotland Yard Gate'.

A 'penthouse' was then a sentry box with a sloping (i.e. 'pent') roof. The comments above, therefore, reveal the likely presence of a Household Cavalry HQ in Scotland Yard occupying Cromwell's refurbished Life Guard of Horse facilities and being guarded by double mounted sentries at its main entrance gate. This latter gate stood where today Great Scotland Yard joins Whitehall and survived until 1818. Interestingly, part of this Scotland Yard area retained the name 'Royal Stable Yard' until some 50 years ago. The Foot Guard sentry's 'penthouse' guarded the entrance to their new administrative HQ, namely at the south end of the Tiltyard, where the public pathway crossed from park to highway. This HQ was adjoined on its south-east corner by the Foot Guards sutlery, open to both military and public alike, hence the need for the sentry.

The Foot Guards sutlery (in common with numerous public and coffee houses) was called the Monck's Head in commemoration of the author of the Restoration: it was to retain this identity until General Monck's death a decade later. After this, the famous, or rather, infamous Tiltyard Coffee House began to develop in conjunction with the sutlery. As mentioned earlier, Edward Lloyd was one early sutler; another contemporary was Richard Washbourne, who issued his own trade tokens 'at the Tiltyard' depicting the bust of General Monck. The Foot Guards' sutler rented his rooms from the commanding officers of the Guards Regiments. However, as the facility became an established place for public refreshment, the sutlery and the coffee house were run as separate businesses with separate managers.[65] Although contracted privately by the commanding officers of the regiments

they served, sutlers could sell their wares to any passing civilians, the sutler was always a civilian trader in the first place and military supplier in the second. In the Horse Guards Tiltyard, for example, the Monck's Head was sited on the old public access lane joining the highway to St James's Park, taking full advantage of any passing trade. These factors were also the beginnings of a unique situation whereby the general public had (by indisputable right of way) access to, and through, a site that was developed and intended solely for military purposes. Not until well into Victoria's reign was this Horse Guards' anomaly to be resolved. A few sutlers were women, and perhaps some of these had a wider entrepreneurial vision than their male counterparts, as the following comment hints: 'Petition by Jane Gerrard (Widow) for a lease of a small piece of ground in the Tiltyard to finish building a house in which to entertain H.M.Guards to which she is continued Sutler in place of her late husband.'[66]

FIRST DUTIES

The logistical problems of quartering the new Household regiments had received initial attention so they could fulfil the role Charles had intended for them: to be readily available to leave their quarters for duty anywhere in the capital and the Home Counties. The Royal Regiment of Horse was not of Household Cavalry status at this time and was quartered at Southwark, but it nevertheless assisted the three Horse Guards Troops in their civil duty role.

Each of these three troops was formed of four squadrons of 50 men, and two squadrons were on duty for one day in every six. The Horse Guards

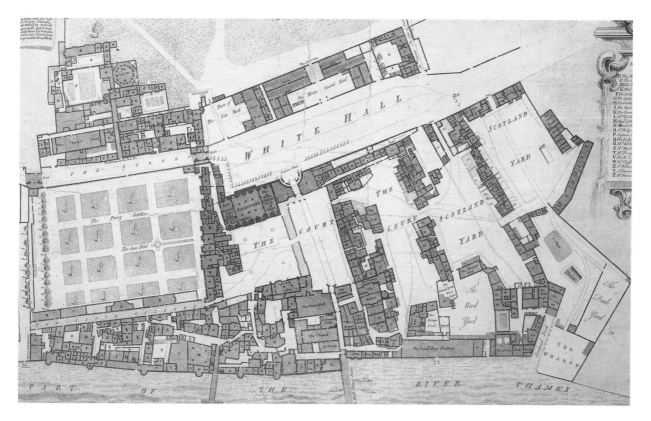

The ground plan of Whitehall Palace, attr. John Fisher, c.1670. The northernmost of the two gates (top right) shown opening from Scotland Yard on to Whitehall is the one where the Accounts for September 1661 record 'setting up two penthouses for the Horse Guard at Scotland Yard Gate.' These two 'penthouses' (sentry boxes) controlled access to the original Household Cavalry HQ located in Scotland Yard from 1661 to April 1664, when the Old Horse Guards building assumed the role and both sentries and the HQ moved over the road – to where they have been ever since. Midway between the Court Gate and Scotland Yard Gate is seen a row of offices. Those marked '27' and listed as belonging to 'Sir John Trevor', later became the Secretary-at-War's temporary 'War Office' when that department moved out of the Old Horse Guards structure in 1710. Sir John Trevor was Secretary of State for the Army 1668–72. (TNA (PRO), MPE1/325)

performed their duties dressed as archetypal cavaliers. All had red coats – the King's Troop with blue facings and gold or silver lace ornamentation – blue velvet carbine belts and red breeches, the whole ensemble topped with wide-brimmed, feather-flaunting hats. The basic colour of Queen Catherine's Troop was the sea green of the duchy of Braganza, while the Duke of York favoured yellow for his guard. But underlining their real role was the pistol-proof 'pott' in the hat, and the back and breast cuirasses worn on every escort duty. This was how they were seen by the three visiting Russian envoys (and Pepys) on one of the earliest recorded Household Cavalry escorts that accompanied the delegation to the official reception at the Guildhall in the City, or to use the great diarist's words, 'for whose reception all the City trained-bands do attend in the streets, and the King's Life-guard'.[67]

The Royal Regiment of Horse secured safe passage on the highways between major military towns and dockyards anywhere in the southern half of the country. Quite often the troops were required to ride, posse-like, around a given locality to quell outbreaks of banditry. The Horse Guards Troops were to have their share of rural law enforcement. In September 1667, they were sent to Winchcombe, Gloucester, 'to spoil the Tobacco there',[68] as Pepys records, a measure designed to protect the government's lucrative Virginia trade and enforce previously ignored statutes.

It is also a throwaway comment of gossip from the inimitable diarist that offers an eyewitness account of the kind of risk encountered by sentries of the Foot Guards Tiltyard Guard, prior to the construction of Old Horse Guards:

> Among other discourse, Mrs. Sarah tells us how the King sups at least four or five times every week with my Lady Castlemayne; and most often stays till the morning with her and goes home through the garden all alone privately, and that so the very Centry's take notice of it and speak of it.[69]

The 'garden' mentioned was the Privy Garden of Whitehall Palace; this covered the area now occupied by the Ministry of Defence building. At least two Foot Guards' 'centrys' from the Tiltyard Guard were posted there on permanent guard to apprehend anyone trying to gain illegal entrance to the royal apartments. These apartments were sited around the north-east perimeter of the garden, while those of 'my Lady Castlemayne' were at this time diagonally opposite in the south-west corner buildings, about opposite where Downing Street now is. In the night-time and early-morning darkness of the garden, the patrolling guard had to take great pains in identifying the king's person from any others who may have been suspect. This Privy Garden guard continued to be mounted from the Tiltyard Guard for most of the next hundred years, although the palace itself would disappear in the fire of 1698.

The management of the unofficial 'army' force overall, not just the Household Troops, posed increasing difficulties. Bombay, and Tangier and its garrison, had been acquired by Charles's marriage to the Portuguese princess Catherine of Braganza. Tangier was a vitally important Mediterranean staging post for troop movements and trade, its role analogous to that of Gibraltar in more recent times. His marriage treaty required Charles to send 2,000 foot soldiers and 500 horse to help maintain Portugal's independence from Spain. Also, just across the Channel in Dunkirk, a motley assemblage of mercenaries and Cromwellian troops stranded there since the battle of the Dunes in 1658 added to the hidden 'army'. Having been ignored by Parliament, they now looked to the restored monarchy to ensure their future. Charles 'solved' his Tangier obligation by sending the Continental force there, augmented by assorted disbanded troops, as two newly raised regiments – The Tangier Horse and The Tangier Regiment. These were later to become, respectively, The Royal Dragoons and the Queen's Royal (West Surrey) Regiment, which in modern times became amalgamated, respectively, into The Blues and Royals, and the Queen's Royal Surrey Regiment.[70]

Like the guard quarters, all the military administration remained Cromwellian, the various offices responsible for provisioning, clothing, ordnance, discipline, pay, etc. being scattered around the Whitehall environs, many in private houses. With the new 'Guards and Garrisons' force now an established fact, plus the other inherited military commitments just noted, it was clearly a common-sense and vital requirement to collect together as many as possible of the disparate Cromwellian command functions, put them under one roof, and so make the general army management up to date and well coordinated. However, Parliament continued to insist that an 'army' *per se* still did not exist.

CONSTRUCTING OLD HORSE GUARDS

In 1663, meetings between the regimental commanders and the staff of the Paymaster of Works, Hugh May, defined the site and the criteria – the Tiltyard would house duty quarters for all the new Household regiments as well as some of the principal military officials. As a site, the Tiltyard still retained the defensive qualities so essential to the Trained Bands 20 years earlier, and to successive forces stationed there since: the security of the Court could be guarded, access to the road to Westminster controlled, the woodland of St James's could be patrolled for threats and, not least, the new army command would be in close contact with the King just across the Whitehall highway.

Approval for the plan was granted, and the Office of Works' minutes record the commencement of the work on 5 August 1663: 'Taking down of the Guard House... Taking coping stones from the brickwalls and stone walls of the Tiltyard ... taking down the Old Guard House in the Tiltyard.'[71] The construction of the new facility took less than a year, the surviving accounts recording, 'Tiltyard... From ye first of September 1663 to ye first of April 1664 ... charges in building Horse and Foot Guards there'.[72] The first Horse Guards building – 'Old Horse Guards' – was completed by the summer of 1664 at a cost of about £4,066-19-1¼, the accounts being incomplete. It was to stand for 90 years, taking its name from the permanent presence there of the duty troops of Charles's Horse Guard.

The architect is not named in the accounts so far as they exist, but supervising the project was Hugh May, Paymaster of Works, who worked under the overall authority of Surveyor General Sir John Denham. The finished design does, perhaps, offer some hints about the architect. All of the new building was in red brick with stone quoins and window mullions, reflecting the influence of the Dutch style on the exiled court and its adherents. Possibly Sir John Denham initiated the design, but as diarist John Evelyn said, he was 'a better poet than an architect'.[73] By virtue of his post, Hugh May must have been closely involved and had designed and built several imposing 'Dutch-style' houses for leading courtiers. Another possible contender is Sir Roger Pratt, who designed various large country estates with very similar designs to Old Horse Guards, namely Kingston Lacey, Horseheath Hall and Clarendon House; all built in brick and stone, with wings projecting from a pedimented central hall block and an enclosed courtyard with entrance lodges.

The reluctance of Parliament to grant anything but minimal funds for military purposes is indicated in the building economies, as revealed in the accounts' comments for Old Horse Guards. For example, Master bricklayer Maurice Emmett records, 'breaking through and making good of xiiij [14] windowes next the Parke'.[74] This implies that the old Tudor wall was retained to enclose the new ground-floor stabling and had window spaces knocked through it. Some confirmation for this seems apparent in the Works entry for 6 August 1663, which speaks only of removing 'coping stones' from the old Tiltyard enclosing walls, namely the brick wall to the Park and the stone wall to Whitehall; demolition of the walls themselves is not apparent in the minutes. The building of new windows in the old wall is described further in another entry: 'Cxv [115] ft. of free stone some new some old about the pinning in of ten windowes to give light to the new stables of the Horse Guard next the Park...'[75]

But the most fatal economy, insofar as the future structural integrity of the building was concerned, appears in John Angier's account for carpenters' work: 'for extraordinary timbr. in iiij [4] paire of great rafters and two beames to carry the walls there'.[76] These latter two 'beames', certainly oak and probably not less than 18 inches square, were mounted with one end on the old Park wall and the other end on the opposite, far stable wall fronting the courtyard on the Whitehall side. Running under each of the two beams was a main entrance to the stable wings to the north and south of the central brickwork tower. Each beam carried the full weight of the brick superstructure above it over the stable doors below. With support from the ground therefore only possible at the beam ends, it was to be only a matter of time before the massive, super-incumbent masonry weight distorted the centre section of these beams and, consequently, progressively disjointed the brickwork above. The other timber listed, the 'iiij paire of great rafters', sat transversely across the beams, providing the roof to the new archway entrance, which allowed carriages for the first time a wide enough access into the Park. A further economy, potentially endangering the tower

masonry, is evidenced by the Works comment, 'cutting away the water tables on both sides for the ['greate'] doores to fall close to the wall'.[77] The 'water tables' referred to were the projecting courses of bricks that ran along the bottom of all the main walling, specifically intended to divert rainwater outwards from wall foundations. By cutting back this course to allow the gates to open 'close to the wall', the drainage system was compromised, making the wall likely to sink under the masonry weight as rainwater seeped unimpeded into its foundations below.

When completed, Old Horse Guards comprised two distinct parts: a 'Horse Guard' and a 'Foot Guard'. For the 'Horse Guard', the layout was much as today's building, having a three-storey central clock tower block with an archway through it to St James's Park and two wings projecting towards Whitehall around a courtyard. The archway was called 'The Park Gate' and had 'great doores' closed each night. On the Whitehall side, the high Tiltyard wall was retained to enclose the courtyard from the highway, but was pierced with a new gateway opposite the archway to give access to the Park. In the wall on either side of this gate was a sentry box for the two Horse Guards mounted sentries. This gate to Whitehall was also closed each night by the 'great gates next the street'. The 'Horse Guard' filled the northern half of the Tiltyard. Most of the remaining area to the south was occupied by the new buildings for the 'Foot Guard', excepting the southern extremity, where the old public lane running from Whitehall to the park was left in place. This small enclosed area of undeveloped Tiltyard was now guarded by official gate-keeper Jervis Price, appointed for life by the Chief Keeper of the Park, the

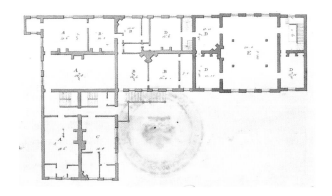

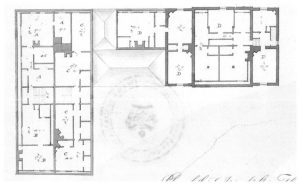

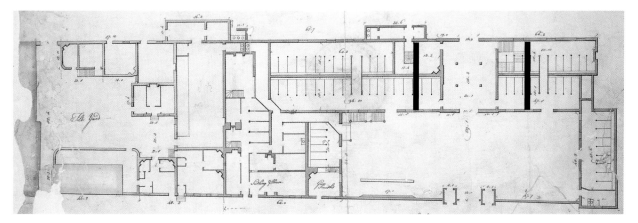

The reason why Old Horse Guards nearly collapsed. These floor plans showing the apportionment of rooms in Old Horse Guards are undated but probably early 1700s. As can be seen on the ground floor plan (bottom), the north and south walls of the central tower supporting structure, which carried the entire tower weight over the arch and stabling below, were not carried down to ground level but instead rested on the 'two beames to carry the walls' which are indicated on the plan in black. These eventually failed under the massive weight of the tower masonry, dislocating the whole structure. First Floor (top left): A. Rooms belonging to the Horse Guards; B. Officers rooms; C. Horse Grenadier's room; D. Rooms & office, belonging to the Judge Advocate; E. The Chapple. Second Floor (top right): A. Pay office to 2nd troop of Guards; B. Pay officer to 1st troop of Guards; C. Apartment belonging to the attendants to officers of Horse Guards; D. The apartments belonging to the Judge Advocate. (TNA (PRO), WORK 30/168–170)

Duke of Albemarle. It was used as an internal parade ground and gave the Foot Guard presence there the identity 'The Tiltyard Guard': it was to mount under this name until November 1898.

Another, more sinister, occupant of this Tiltyard area was the 'wooden horse'. Continued from Cromwellian times (it is described in 1644)[78], it was a military punishment comprising wooden boards on edge which offenders were required to 'ride', often with leg weights attached, for the period of their sentence. A typical punishment was that imposed on Thomas Hanslope by court martial on 4 June 1666, 'that he do ride the Wooden Horse for six days together during the time of the mounting of the Guard, having his crimes written upon his breast and back'.[79] The luckless Hanslope also had to 'run the Gauntelop [a gauntlet of whips] and be Cashier'd', and all for the offence of 'speaking mutinous and opprobrious words' against his commander, Sir Thomas Daniell. The nearby public path across the residual Tiltyard area ensured additional humiliation from civilian passers-by. The wooden horse certainly

continued in use through to the Georgian era, a new one being installed (for £3-12-0)[80] in 1713, while further references are found as late as 1827 when its use was still being 'deprecated'.[81]

No illustration exists to show Old Horse Guards immediately on its completion; the earliest illustration of it by S. Rawle is dated 1677. Seen from St James's Park, Old Horse Guards stands with its clock tower projecting prominently above the adjoining buildings of Whitehall Palace. To the right foreground, the Foot Guards guardroom is clearly visible with, to the right, the ornate Park Stairs leading down from the Tiltyard Gallery. Contemporary with Rawle's illustration is the ground plan of the whole palace c.1670 attributed to John Fisher (p.41). Here the ground-floor stable plan of Old Horse Guards is clearly seen towards the top, alongside the Whitehall thoroughfare. The central arch and courtyard are visible with, in the latter, a 'drinking pond' for the horses. The stabling is depicted in stylized form; there was, in fact, room for 108 horses. The Foot Guard quarters are separated to

the south by a passageway and some rooms described on the plan as 'For the Sutler'. Another view (p.37) by H. Danckerts, also c.1674, shows Old Horse Guards as the background to a view of King Charles walking with his courtiers in St James's Park. Immediately behind the royal party, the Tiltyard Guard is seen turned out on parade with its Colour, being found by the Duke of Albemarle's Regiment of Foot Guards, today the Coldstream Guards. The entrance to their guardroom is behind the sentry on duty.

It is interesting to note the size of the gravelled area between Old Horse Guards and the grassland of the park. Originally a confluence of public tracks from St James's to King Street, its usage by, successively, the mounted knights awaiting to enter the Tiltyard, then parades of Cromwell's Life Guards, followed by the drills and guard mountings of Charles's Horse Guards and 'Tiltyard Guard', all combined to level the area: creating the precursor of today's Horse Guards Parade. Interestingly, today, a decision has been made to cease the Household

Cavalry Queen's Life Guard Mounting in the courtyard on the Whitehall side and conduct it instead on the Parade on the Park side. Thus it returns, geographically, to its Restoration origins. When newly built, virtually the entire ground floor of Old Horse Guards was allocated to stabling for 108 horses of the Horse Guard, with adjoining blacksmith's and gunsmith's forges and workshops. The rooms for the guard on duty occupied the first floor to the south of the clock tower and comprised the Great Guard Room, officers' rooms, 'Briggadier's Room' and Commissary's Office. In the Restoration Household Cavalry, a 'briggadier' fulfilled corporal status, but confusingly, the post was held by Lieutenants of Horse; thus, their 'room' could be said to be for junior officers.[82] The 'Commissary's Office' housed Sir Thomas Clarges who, as Commissary General, was responsible for the general provisioning of all the newly raised armed forces. The central room over the gateway was a chapel. In the 1662 Articles of War, Charles II had insisted, 'the Chaplains to the Troops of Guards shall every day read the Common Prayers of the Church of England to the soldiers respectively under their charge ... every officer or soldier absent from Prayres shall for every absence lose a day's pay to his Majesty.'[83]

Surrounding the chapel were the extensive chambers of the Judge Advocate General, Sir Edmund Pierce. On the second floor were separate pay offices for each of the duty troops, and rooms of the officer's attendants, with all remaining space being allocated to the Judge Advocate's clerks. Here, too, were the Provost Martial's officers, with one provost martial (marshal) for each Household regiment, the Life

Guards' one defined as Marshal to the Horse. Finally, the attic storey housed the forage store, hayloft, granary and other equipment storerooms. The north wing of Old Horse Guards, above a small stable area conceded to the Horse Guard guard, was entirely given over to the Paymaster General's offices and included his grace and favour living quarters.

The Foot Guards' wing occupying the south of the Tiltyard was mostly single storey and provided accommodation for some 50 duty soldiers. Separate orderly rooms existed for the 1st Foot Guards and Coldstreams, and later the Scots Guards. As in the Horse Guards, the officers and NCOs had separate rooms; in fact, the Foot Guards' Officer's Room was

Close-up pencil sketch of Old Horse Guards from Rawle's view of c.1677. Of unknown origin, this sketch provides much finer detail of the building's park frontage, e.g. Charles II's coat of arms in the pediment. The high-pitched roof with lantern tower in the left background is Cardinal Wolsey's Great Hall built in 1528 when the ecclesiastical palace was still called York Place. It survived to 1698. (Author's collection)

used on occasion for court martial hearings.[84] The south-east of the Foot Guards' wing was taken up by the sutler, who expanded into basement, ground and first-floor rooms. The Horse Guards' sutler had rooms in the north wing under the Paymaster, and still has rooms in that wing today.

The two mounted Household Cavalry duty sentries at Old Horse Guards stood guard opposite the Court Gate in Whitehall in the boxes – or vedettes, to give them their correct name – as indeed they continue to do so to the present day. At the same time, dismounted sentries patrolled the courtyard and attended to the security of the main gates into the park and also the main entrance to their duty guardroom. This was situated on the first floor, at the top of 'the Great Stair', which led down into the courtyard on the Whitehall side, immediately to the south of the central archway.

Some duty vernacular regarding these sentries has also descended to modern times in that the dismounted sentries pacing back and forth under the arch, between the two main gates, are still called the 'Gate Sentries'. Today, they actively protect the office entrances to the building as well as maintaining public order within all of Horse Guards' environs, which technically still extends to any part of the Parade Ground (see p.125). The single sentry patrolling under the north arcade has watch over the access to the guards' administrative and duty quarters. Because the carbines of the guard were stored nearby, he was called the 'Sentry over the Arms', and is still so called today. This particular sentry's regular pacing up and down behind the arcade columns has given rise to comparisons with chicken enclosures where the fowls similarly pace back and forth along the line of their caging. Thus, a slang term exists that when this sentry is on duty, he is 'in the chicks'. Some attempts have been made to identify this slang term with the actual presence of chicks relating to a vaulted cellar underneath Horse Guards which, it has been assumed, was formerly used as a cock-fighting arena. The cellar tale is a well-established tradition, though documentary proof of its use is still wanting. It may have had such use on *ad hoc* occasions, but with the relentless search for more office space it was never a permanent feature. Also, there is no apparent connection between the Sentry over the Arms and the possible use of immature gaming fowls ('chicks') in the room below ground – only trained adult fowls fought and were bet upon in cockpits.

The central clock tower of Old Horse Guards was fitted with a clock made by Thomas Herbert, and it commenced the tradition of being the most accurate public clock in London: today's Georgian Horse Guards continued in the role of timekeeper to the capital until the advent of Big Ben to the south of Whitehall in 1858. Although Herbert's name is not apparent in the surviving accounts, his claim to being the Old Horse Guards clockmaker is recorded in the Lord Chamberlain's records for later in the century, where at a hearing about royal clocks, the following appears in the committee minutes:

Mr. Herbert the Clockmaker remembers but four Great Clocks made for the Crown Since he had the Place [i.e. royal clockmaker] which were all made by him. 2 of them viz. St. James's and the Tower were made by the Ld. Chamberlain Warrants to him which are Still extant. Two others viz. for the Horse Guard and for Kensington, he affirms were made by order of K. Charles ye 2nd and of the late Queen.[85]

Mr Herbert's clock had a single hand and struck the hours on a single bell, probably cast at London's oldest bell foundry at Whitechapel.

St James's Park and Old Horse Guards

St James's Park was used by the public during the early years of Charles' reign, but regular patrols by the newly installed troops at Old Horse Guards kept the nearby palace free of loiterers of criminal intent. Typical was one Edward Byshaw who, acting in a suspicious manner within the park, 'was seized by a party of Monk's Life Guard and with little notice had to pack up and come to the Horse Guard'.[86] The Household troops were to serve the metropolis as a police force called out to civil disorders until the advent of Sir Robert Peel's police force in 1829. Also, as reparation, many hundreds of disbanded Cromwellian soldiers worked in the Park as labourers. One principal construction was the laying of a large underground conduit from the Thames, which ran under both King Street and Old Horse Guards, and eventually emerged in the Park; this kept the ponds there topped up at times of exceptionally high tides. The sluice gate controlling the flow stood near the north side of Horse Guards Parade and survived to Victorian times.

Allowing the general public access to the Park would clearly impinge upon the King's new-found social freedom; therefore, shortly after the construction of Old Horse Guards, he restricted entry to those with official permission only. The Lord Chamberlain's office advised the sentries of a codeword that they were to request from all persons wishing to enter the Park. 'The Word' was changed weekly and was communicated secretly to the guard commanders. Even Pepys was locked out on occasion: 'At Whitehall I could not get into the Park and so was fain to stay in the gallery over the [Holbein] gate to look into the passage into the Park into which the King hath forbid of late anybody's coming.'[87] This regulation exists unchanged to the present day, as far as access to the Park through Horse Guards is concerned. At 10pm every night, the Horse Guards gates are locked until 6am the following morning. During this period, only repetition of the correct word in response to the sentry's challenge will allow the visitor access. The annual twilight ceremonial of 'Beating the Retreat' on Horse Guards Parade early in June by the Household Cavalry and Foot Guards traces its origins to this evening closing of the garrison gates.

Apart from selected courtiers, the only persons allowed a privileged use of the Park were the keepers. In fact, it was a perk of the senior ranger to graze cows there and to supplement his income by selling milk to the houses that backed on to the Park. Later, when controlled by the Lord Chamberlain's office, the St James's Milk Fair, as it had become known, was to continue to 1922. Farm animal usage of St James's Park continued until modern times, sheep being grazed there as recently as the summer of 1939.[88]

Restrictions were also placed on the coaches permitted through Horse Guards arch. A radical tightening of palace security occurs in the official records in 1667:

Orders for Coaches – It is his Majesties express pleasure and command that no coaches be permitted to pass into St. James's Park but his own, and the Queen's and the Royal familyes Coaches, and that none be permitted to ride with saddle horses in the sd. Park but the troops of Guard that are appointed to attend his Majesty and the Royal Family: and the officers of the Guards and keepers of the sd. Park are to take care that this order be strictly observed. Given under my hand this 23rd day of June 1667.[89]

This regulation also persists to the present day in that no person, except when specifically authorized by the sovereign, is allowed to drive through Horse Guards archway in any vehicle. Anyone attempting to do so without authorization will be stopped by the sentries.

The Foot Guards' Tiltyard Guard assumed a new responsibility from the spring of 1663, when King Charles's brother James, Duke of York, set up his court in the newly refurbished St James's Palace. A duty detachment of the Guard was allotted for sentry duty outside the then secondary palace. As we will see, this role was promoted from secondary to primary when the King's court was moved from Whitehall to St James's in 1698: the Foot Guards' guard over this national seat of royal court authority has continued at St James's ever since.

A FIRST MILITARY HEADQUARTERS

General Monck had been appointed Commander-in-Chief (C-in-C), but because Parliament recognized the new regiments only as Household protective troops and not as an army *per se*, no accommodation was specified in Old Horse Guards for a general command structure,

only for the Guards commanders. Monck, therefore, had to resort to some ingenuity to effectively control his forces. How he initially accomplished this in *c.*1663–64 was later described by an observant courtier: 'I happened to be the first person that told the Duke of Ormond of Lord Albemarle's pretence to command, having by chance seen an order of that Lord's nailed up at the Horse Guards, whereby he gave general directions to all troops.'[90] This describes probably the earliest example of overall central military command being identified with the Horse Guards building, as opposed to just the Household Troops there. Where, as noted earlier, civilian notices of importance to the general public were pasted on the Court Gate, so in like manner, the general military became used to their orders appearing on Horse Guards' door. That Monck's method was effective is shown by its continuance many years later. In 1691, during the purge of Jacobites, diarist Narcissus Luttrell observed, 'An order is fixt on the Horse Guards door by Whitehall, that no suspected person be permitted to walk in St. James's Park; and that several private doors into it should be shutt up.'[91]

Though it originally controlled just the Household Troops, Old Horse Guards can surely still lay claim to being the nation's first custom-built military administration headquarters. On the stone fronts of the sentry boxes at Horse Guards, one can still see the metal fastenings that once held in place the notice boards on which were pasted proclamations and other notices of public importance. For centuries, Horse Guards has been a place where people would come to read the latest important state communications there displayed.

As C-in-C, Monck did have a personal Secretary-at-War, Sir William Clarke; however, for some years

Clarke did little more than compile minutes and drafts of executive meetings held in Monck's office in the old Cockpit (today, Downing Street). At the outset, there was no designated War Office, but because all initial military control emanated from the C-in-C's office, wherever he happened to work became identified as the 'War Office'. Following Clarke's death while abroad with Monck in June 1666, his deputy Matthew Lock succeeded as Secretary-at-War. Monck recommended him as 'long one of his secretaries, and well versed in army business'.[92]

In 1665, the old 'Green' by the south end of Horse Guards was witness to some extraordinary proclamations. At 10am on 4 March, the heralds faced the Court Gate, and after a fanfare from their attendant state trumpeters, formally announced the declaration of war at sea with the Dutch nation.[93] On 14 June, the heralds' procession returned to the 'Green' to announce a national Thanksgiving Day for a major victory over the Dutch on 3 June.[94] Then, on 26 July, the proclamation was made 'by the officers of Arms, habited in their tabards' for the evacuation from London of the Exchequer Office to Nonsuch House near Epsom to escape the ravages of the Great Plague. The office was not to return to Whitehall until 20 January 1666.[95]

OLD HORSE GUARDS FROM THE PEN OF SAMUEL PEPYS

The King's Guard at Old Horse Guards continued uninterrupted during the plague months though the King and his court had left the capital in May, first for Hampton Court, then Salisbury and, later, Oxford. The royal entourage eventually returned permanently to Whitehall on 1 February 1666.[96] In 1665, Samuel Pepys traced the sinister invasion of the deadly infection through the environs of Old Horse Guards:

I whiled away some time in Westminster – in my way observing several plague-houses in Kings Street and the Palace. (28 June)
From thence walked around to Whitehall, the park being quite locked up. (5 July) [Namely, by 'the Great Doores' at Old Horse Guards described above.]
But Lord, to see how the plague spreads; it being now all over Kings-street. (20 July)

Pepys and his family evacuated to Woolwich in July, not returning to London until early December. However, his curiosity getting the better of him, he could not resist the occasional trip up river to see the desolation for himself; he left for us a record of the miserable scene that the sentries at Old Horse Guards kept watch over: 'But Lord, what a sad time it is, to see no boats upon the River – and grass grows all up and down Whitehall-court – and nobody but poor wretches in the streets.' (20 September)

Although Pepys records at various times the activities of the new Household troops, most unfortunately for us he makes no record at all of the construction of Old Horse Guards. He must have seen the building work as he walked past Old Horse Guards on his regular visits to Whitehall. Furthermore, from the spring of 1664 onwards, he must have frequently seen it as a completed building, as he walked with his friends from Whitehall into St James's Park, through the new arch of Old Horse Guards. Surprisingly, amid his voluminous London

A view of Whitehall in 1713, depicting the gun platform set up in 1688. During the Civil War a gun platform was sited in the ground floor of the Privy Gallery next to the Holbein Gate in 1643, aimed towards the Charing Cross approach. After the rebuilding of the Privy Gallery in 1685, a new gun platform was installed during the Jacobite insurrection, which is the one depicted here to the right of the view. It was finally demolished in 1723. The guns in the original platform were called minions, of 3¼ in. bore, and fired a 5lb ball through an 8ft barrel. After the reign of James II, the guns appear to have only been used ceremonially for firing charges in St James's Park – a role today undertaken by the RHA in Hyde Park – but after 1723 just small 'potts' with charges were retained for the purpose. (H. Terasson, © Queen's Printer and Controller of HMSO, 2005. UK Government Art Collection)

locality detail, other than a brief comment about a fire there in November 1666, there is no Diary entry whatever about the building.

Pepys's silence on the subject is, in itself, a telling comment on the prospect of the new 'flying army', as he perceived the Household Troops.[97] Two reasons can be suggested for his making no record of this striking new building in Whitehall. Pepys had spent all his life up to his mid-twenties living in London under the rigours of the socially repressive Cromwellian regime. The prospect of a new military authority making its presence unequivocally known in his favourite Whitehall campus would have been something of an anathema to him. His response seems to have been to ignore it completely, at least insofar as his diary is concerned. He must have regarded Old Horse Guards as no more than a new, ornate entry into St James's Park. The other reason relates to his perception of architecture. Pepys could appraise a grand house in its setting, but generally he didn't look at buildings along a street with a critical eye.[98] He seemed to accept them as part of the background, and so not worthy of diary comment. Perhaps he treated the advent of Old Horse Guards in this way.

But even allowing for the foregoing conjecture, Pepys (archetypal wheeler-dealer as he was) remains on record as being on close terms with some of the most senior Household Cavalry officers of the day. Pepys's influence with the officers is evident in his promotion of his errant brother-in-law Balty (Balthasar St Michel) into the Duke of Albemarle's Troop of His Majesty's Life Guard, commanded by Sir Philip Howard. In 1665, when Albemarle was the Duke of York's deputy as Admiral of the Kingdom, Pepys' naval administrative skills often helped Albemarle out of a tight spot. Consequently, on 19 October 1665, Pepys writes, 'After dinner... I went to the Duke of Albemarle and among other things spoke to him for my wife's brother Balty to be of his Guard, which he kindly answered that he should'.[99] By 4 December, Pepys's insistence had seen Balty 'put as right hand man, and with other marks of special respect'.[100] By April 1666, Balty was on the move again after Pepys found him a post as naval muster-master (i.e. crew procurement). Pepys again used his Court seniority to keep Balty on the Guards' payroll while employed with the Navy. To do so he had to 'wait on Sir Philip Howard about suffering my wife's brother to go to sea, and to save his pay with the Duke's guards – which, after a little difficulty, he did with great respect agree to'.[101] Balty went to sea on 28 April, Pepys happily recording, 'it will be worth £100 this year to him, beside keeping him the benefit of his pay in the guard'.[102]

Though flagrantly using Guards' funds to further his own interests, it seems that on at least one occasion (24 March 1668), Pepys visited the guard at Old Horse Guards:

Having done here, I out and met Sir Fr.Hollis … he took Lord Brouncker and me down to the guards, he and his company being upon the guards today; and there he did, in a handsome room to that purpose, make us drink, and did call for his Bagpiper; which with pipes of ebony tipped with silver, he did play beyond anything of that kind that ever I heard in my life.[103]

From this encounter, one can infer that perhaps Pepys visited the Foot Guards' Tiltyard Guard rather than the Household Cavalry Guard, the 'handsome room' possibly being the Officers' Room used for courts martial mentioned previously. Which regiment found the guard that day we are left to guess.

In November 1666, a serious fire occurred at Old Horse Guards in a forage store in the north wing. According to the *London Gazette*, 'the timely help which his Majesty and His Royal Highness caused to be applied' prevented the fire from consuming the entire building. Pepys heard, 'part of it blown up with gunpowder',[104] but whether this happened by design or accident is unclear. The eventual repair bill amounted to £625, the blame placed on 'a drunken groom in the hayloft'.

Pepys records many of the activities of Charles II's Household Troops, so it is appropriate that he now bows out of this story with a final comment describing how, after kissing Nell Gwynne at the King's House theatre, he came across, 'at Temple Bar the Guards of Horse in the street, the occasion being that the seamen are in a meeting which put me into a great fright'.[105]

Another diarist, John Evelyn, allows us a glance into an interesting aspect of royal life at Restoration Whitehall which provided a rather unusual duty for the

Household Cavalry. On 19 July 1664, Evelyn visited Whitehall 'to see the event of the Lottery, which his Majestie had permitted Sir Arthur Slingsby to set up for one day in the Banqueting House'. In later times (from 1709 to 1826), it would be a regular duty for Household Cavalry escorts to leave Horse Guards to protect the lottery wheel, stored by the south of the Banqueting House, in its transit to the Guildhall for the annual draw.[106] Evelyn, meanwhile, was unimpressed: 'I gaining onely a trifle, as well did the King, Queene Consort, & Q.Mother for neere 30 lotts: which was thought to be contriv'd very unhandsomely by the master of it, who was in truth a meer shark!'[107]

THE HORSE GUARDS WAR OFFICE

On 1 January 1670, George Monck, Duke of Albemarle, died. His troop of the Horse Guard was renamed to become the Queen's Troop, thereby automatically placing it next to the King's Troop in precedence and reverting the Duke of York's Troop to last in seniority, much to James's annoyance. As far as Old Horse Guards was concerned, a more interesting consequence was that the post of Commander-in-Chief was left vacant. Orders to the Army from the King were henceforth passed to the civil Secretary-at-War, now Matthew Lock, for executive action.

On the assumption of his enhanced role, Lock, a civilian, took the significant step of obtaining an office in Old Horse Guards, thus causing the first juxtaposition there of civil and military control of the armed forces. For his peacetime salary of £1 a day, Lock and his four clerks had ultimate control of all military orders, the Board of General Officers, discipline, clothing, recruiting, the Paymaster's establishments, Treasury warrants, the Commissary General of Musters, the Judge Advocate General, and Irish troop establishments and movements. He was not personally answerable to Parliament for any of these responsibilities, but only to the Secretary of State. Thus, above all else 'Mr. Lock's Office', as frequently mentioned in the Works accounts, can be viewed as the first Horse Guards War Office.

In 1670, a plot hatched by Captain Mason and 50 men 'from the old army'[108] to assassinate the king by attacking the guards at Whitehall gates was foiled. An interesting parallel to Essex's plot some 70 years before, this failed too, but it changed some of the guard arrangements at the Tiltyard. The powder store still in the Cromwellian gun battery adjoining the Holbein Gate was closed down. The gunpowder was removed to a basement store under the Foot Guards' quarters in the Tiltyard to become a supply point to other London and Home Counties garrisons. There it was replenished by the Tower of London at an average rate of 20 barrels a month. Another accounts entry reveals that the more basic means of defence was not overlooked either: 'mending ye shades with new deales at the Foot Guard, that keepes the Pikes from rusting'.[109] The Foot Guards' pikes were stacked in racks against the outside walls for quick access if needed and 'ye shades' were the sloping wooden deal tops which kept the rain off the rack.

After the Household Troops, the largest allocation of rooms at Old Horse Guards in the 1670s was for the Paymaster General and his staff, which took up most of the northern wing. Next came the Commissary's department responsible for the provisioning and supply of the army, and integrated with the Ordnance department for the control of armaments. Then the Judge Advocate's chambers, utilizing a suite of rooms adjacent to the central chapel; and finally Secretary-at-War, Matthew Lock, with his three rooms and four clerks. The post of Judge Advocate General (JAG) has its origins in the reign of Elizabeth, with a civil judge to conduct courts martial; after the Restoration, the legal appointment of the JAG was required to prepare the Crown's prosecution case, arrange court martial administration, and present the findings of general courts martial before the sovereign. The sovereign then passed his confirmation, mitigation or commutation of sentence back through the JAG's office to the offender's regiment for enactment. The JAG's office, however, was involved to some degree in the documentation for all versions of court martial – General, Field, Regimental, District or Garrison – the JAG himself was only required in person to attend General courts martial, these being held mostly in the Old Horse Guards Great Room.[110] The JAG or his deputy was also expected to attend the meetings of the Board of General Officers held at Old Horse Guards. These meetings, apart from their original purpose to regulate the clothing of the army, grew to cover a virtually limitless range of points of military dissent, mostly against the civil authorities.[111] As a consequence it was with considerable reluctance that the JAG gave up room space to the expanding Secretary-at-War's department.

During Charles II's reign, the new military force grew proportionately to the roles assigned to it, which was, in the main, the policing of the new colonies around the world. But Secretary-at-War Lock ran a tight ship when it came to his office stationery keeping up with these new administrative demands, his

expenses for 1674 amounting to just £14-19-0, included in which were 'seven best penknives', '1300 large Dutch quills', 'four duble bottles of inke', and, not least, 'six rullers' at fourpence each.[112] Interestingly another cost to the public purse occurs at this time for 'Making a pulpit at ye Horse Guard for ye Chaplain there 4ft 6" high; 2ft 4" square with a floore to it and a deske before.'[113] Presumably an original pulpit once existed – one wonders how it got worn out?

In February 1673 an early Continental deployment of the Household Cavalry occurred, when a composite troop of 150 men (including additionally John Morgridge, kettle-drummer, the 1st Foot Guards) went to France for action in the Netherlands. They found the action at the siege of Maastricht the same year. Alongside them fought a certain Monsieur D'Artagnan of the King's Musketiers, later to be immortalized by the author Alexandre Dumas. They came home in 1674.

The establishment of the Horse Guards troops was augmented in 1678 by the addition of a detachment of the newly formed Horse Grenadiers to each troop. John Evelyn thought them 'a new sort of dragoons, who carried also granados & were habited after the Polish manner with long picked caps very fierce and fantastical; & was very exotic'.[114] However, Ann Richards, 'purveyor to the King's Guard of Horse', queried, 'will her expenses be increased in providing neccessaries, fire and candle etc, for the Guards since adding of the Grenadiers to them?' They were, from 4/- a day to 9/6 a day, 'and the King will allow that there be 5 fires in all, 3 for the Horse Guards, 2 for the Horse Grenadiers'.[115] It is interesting that the Foot Guards' sutler is always referred to as such, but the sutler to the Household Cavalry is invariably called a 'purveyor'. Of interest too is the appearance of these Horse Grenadiers in Rooker's view of Horse Guards, *c*.1763, (title page), evidently performing duty as members of the King's Life Guard in their distinctive mitre caps. Their 'grenades' were supplied to both the Horse Grenadier Guards and to the grenadier companies of the Foot Guards from Captain Thomas Sylver's ordnance store and armoury.

In 1678, a further safety measure came into being whereby the colonels of the three troops of Horse Guards were ordered to act as the king's personal bodyguard and 'to stay next to the King's person before all others ... from his rising to his going to bed'.[116] Each of the colonels was to perform this office month by month alternately, the colonel on duty signifying his responsibility by carrying a gold-headed staff. The 'Gold Stick-in-Waiting', as the duty colonel became known, was deputized on occasion by his subordinate regimental commanding officer who carried a silver-headed staff denoting his office. These offices of state continue unchanged today with the Colonels of The Life Guards and The Blues and Royals taking the duty month by month in turn. The Treasury records describe the creation of the original actual Gold Stick: 'Monsieur St. Gille Vannier to be paid his bill for a gold stick for the Captain of the Horse Guards which he carries when he waits upon His Majesty ... £22.7.10'.[117]

THE HORSE GUARDS ARMOURY

The closing years of Charles's reign were marked by increasing political turmoil. One consequence of this was the decision, in October 1682, to create an armoury at Old Horse Guards:

Whereas we find it requisite and necessary for the Good of our Service that a Train of Artillery of Brass Ordnance be forthwith provided in readiness with all fitting Equipage thereunto belonging in order to the better Defence of our Royal Person and preserving the peace of our Kingdom in these Seditious and troublesome times... And We do further will and require you to cause a convenient Roome or Roomes for an Armoury to be prepared within our Guardhouse near St. James's Park for the lodging of a Competent number of Offensive and Defensive Armes as well for Foot as Horse to be in readiness for our Service and defence upon any occasion And likewise that you appoint a Sufficient person to be Storekeeper of the said Armoury... Given at our Court at Whitehall the 5th December 1682... To our Rt.trusty and Welbeloved George Lord Dartmouth Mast.General of Our Ordnance.[118]

In November 1682, an order was issued 'to Thos.Sylver Master Gunner at Whitehall, to sett Carpenters and other Artificers at work to fitt up ye upper room over ye Horseguards at Whitehall for an Armoury according to ye direction of ye Mty. Survey'.[119] Exactly which 'upper room' remains unclear. Probably sited south of the central tower block and clearly quite sizeable for, as well as holding the ordnance ordered as above, on 19 December 1682 delivery was also taken of 'ye number of 1000 swords to ye new Armoury at Whitehall'.[120]

The armoury was likely sited to the south; to the north of the central tower was housed the workshop of John Shaw, gunsmith to their Majesty's Guards. This adjoined the office later used by Secretary-at-War William Blathwaite, who took exception to the

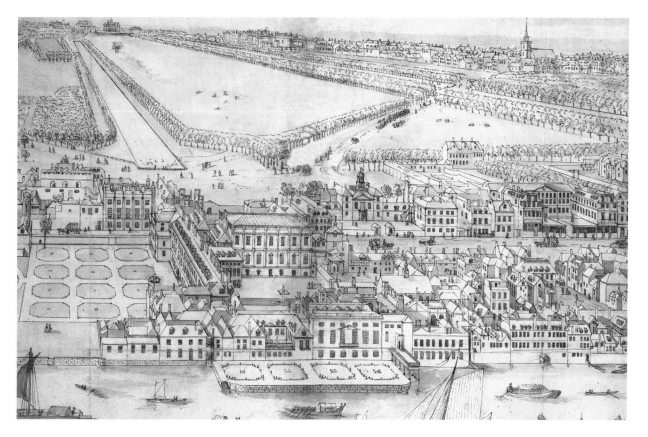

Bird's-eye view of Whitehall Palace, c.1695. A three-dimensional version of Fisher's plan some 20 years on. Old Horse Guards is clearly seen at centre right, with its now massive self-contained northern wing for the Paymaster constructed in 1693. A relic of Queen Mary's 'terras' garden, seen projecting into the river and built by Wren in 1693–94, survives today behind the Ministry of Defence. Also by Wren, and seen abutting the south end of the Banqueting House (centre), is his vast new Privy Gallery block of 1685–86. The Parade Ground is already well on its way to its present size. On the extreme left is the start of Lord Arlington's coachway to Arlington House. From top right, the Mall runs across the entire park also to Arlington House, just visible. (L. Knyff, Westminster City Archives)

'smoake, noyse and danger' associated with Shaw's work and petitioned that he be given 'the hire of a Shop further off'.[121] Clearly any pre-existing armoury premises to the north would have also been suspect to the fastidious Blathwaite.

The Horse Guards armoury was constructed to house only small arms and their associated ammunition; the larger ordnance was kept at the Gun House sited a little to the north of Horse Guards facing on to the Parade. Here was the Whitehall Master Gunner's official residence and the quarters of the ten or so duty gunners

assigned as the Whitehall gun detachment. The last guns sited at Whitehall for offensive purposes are seen clearly in Terasson's view of *c.*1713 (p.52); these were removed in 1723, and subsequent smaller guns were used in St James's Park only for ceremonial salutes.

The addition of the armoury made the problem of overcrowding even more critical; in fact, the building repair accounts from this time onwards clearly show the structure of Horse Guards suffering from housing considerably more people than it had been designed to accommodate. The replacement of large areas of floorboards, for instance, became almost a monthly occurrence. Also, to provide heating in the many subdivided rooms, new chimney flues were cut into walls and roofs in places not originally designed for them. A parsimonious Treasury, however, kept its corporate eyes averted from the problems of Horse Guards' disjointing masonry.

AN ARMY SPY; AND A NOTABLE SECRETARY

In 1681–82, Sir George Downing (1623–84) was granted permission to extend his property, Hampden House, by the construction of 'new and more houses further westward … abutting upon the wall of St. James's Park on the West side, subject to the proviso that it [the development] be not built any nearer than 14 feet of the wall of the said Park at the West end thereof'.[122] Thus was the genesis of the Downing Street government complex so familiar today. Some verbal traditions survive relating that Downing also set out Horse Guards Parade as part of his property extension.[123] The creation of the parade ground space has been described above; additionally, the Treasury building contract strictly established that Sir George was required to keep his houses outside the Park wall and no closer than 14 feet to it. Consequently, only the back gardens of his Downing Street houses ran up to the Park Wall, set out more or less as they are today. Sir George made no further developments near the Parade prior to his death in July 1684; in fact, his only connection to the military was a dubious period as Intelligence Officer with Cromwell in 1649. His subsequent career under Charles II was as a banker (and part-time spy) with few friends – and his only connection with Horse Guards Parade was to keep his development well clear of it. Adjoining William Kent's later Treasury, Downing's houses continue to enclose the south-western corner of the Parade.

In August 1683 William Blathwaite purchased the post of Secretary-at-War from Matthew Lock. Cometh the hour, cometh the man! Blathwaite's term of office (1683–1704) encompassed the military demands of the Monmouth Rebellion, James II's deposition, the Fire of Whitehall, the Dutch army in England, and the wars of William III – all of which he took in his administrative stride. Blathwaite was to be to the Army what Pepys was to the Navy. From his lodgings in Scotland Yard (granted by the King in 1675) he continued in his post as auditor at the nearby Plantation Office where trade with the colonies was controlled but, at the same time, he kept on Lock's rooms in Old Horse Guards. However, his 'War Office' base until 1689 was his Scotland Yard office. In 1689 he separated these two functions by purchasing for himself a property at Little Wallingford House, abutting the Paymaster's office in the north wing of Old Horse Guards; from here he exercised his Secretary-at-War role. Thus, commuting along Whitehall, Blathwaite managed, virtually single-handedly, the affairs of the army and, as well, much of the colonies, with consummate organizational skill. His job security was unassailable and, as a consequence, he often deemed that the papers of the department were, *ex officio*, his personal property; luckily, by that chance, some still survive in his private collections and so allow us a rare glimpse of a 17th-century Secretary-at-War at work.[124] On the occasions when Blathwaite accompanied the monarch on trips abroad, the Judge Advocate General was sworn in as locum Secretary-at-

War, but only as a figurehead: in fact the War Office – both Old Horse Guards and Little Wallingford House – continued to function independently of the JAG under its Second Clerk, John Thurston. Its Chief Clerk, Adam Cardonnel, always accompanied the travelling Blathwaite as Military Secretary. William Blathwaite was by far the most diligent and organized military administrator to be associated with the Old Horse Guards army headquarters. What is perhaps his most notable surviving memorial exists in his army bed and board 'Domesday' survey – *Abstract of a Particular Account of all the Inns, Ale Houses, etc, in England, with their Stable-Room and Bedding* – compiled in 1686. Co-ordinated from Old Horse Guards and running to 660 pages of entries, it lists all the towns and villages which had public houses capable of housing men and horses on the march. As such, it represented a substantial administrative advance on the previous hit-and-miss method of feeding and resting an army on the move. Only some 20,000 public beds were identified across the country – possibly enough for the peacetime establishment, but woefully inadequate for a country on a war footing. But at least Blathwaite had taken an important step in the right direction.[125]

Charles II died at his beloved Whitehall on 6 February 1685, having spent his last months, writes diarist John Evelyn, 'very melancholic, not stirring without redoubled guards'.[126]

JAMES II'S CATHOLIC CALAMITY

Diarist John Evelyn attended the heraldic pageantry and colourful splendour of an accession proclamation on 'the Green' to the south of Horse Guards the following day:

We first went to Whitehall Gate about ten of the clock, where accompanied with Four of His Majesties Serjeants of Arms, Eight Trumpets, and Two Marshals-Men, all on Horseback fronting the Court-Gate, the Lancaster Herald (after the Kettle Drums and Trumpets had thrice sounded) Read the said Proclamation, and which was thereupon Proclaimed aloud by Richmond Herald...[127]

Almost immediately, James II (r.1685–88) started to impose his strict interpretations of the monarchy with its underlying Catholic ideals. As a starting point, he appointed Sir Christopher Wren to rebuild the old Privy Gallery, adding a Roman Catholic chapel at its western extremity. This new Privy Gallery, on the same site as the old, closely resembled the blocks of the present Royal Hospital at Chelsea; internally, it was sumptuously decorated with black and white marble, ceilings by Verrio, and carvings by Grinling Gibbons and Arnold Quellin. The queen's suites of rooms alongside the river were also reconstructed in a building programme that was to extend some years beyond James's reign. The completed scheme can be seen in the view of Whitehall of *c*.1695 by Leonard Knyff. Old Horse Guards was not included in the plans, but Wren's opinion was sought on the question of re-surfacing the road crossing St James's Park from Arlington House to Old Horse Guards. (Arlington House became Buckingham Palace in a later reign.)

The Duke of Monmouth's rebellion to dethrone James failed miserably in July 1685. James thought the failure of the Protestant duke was indicative of an increasing, underlying support for his Catholic designs; he was to be proved fatally wrong. Meanwhile, he used this pretext to increase his army with solely Catholic units, one such being a fourth Troop of Horse Guards commanded by the ardently Catholic Lord Dover. At the same time, senior Protestant officers were prematurely 'retired' from their commands, which came to include the colonel of the Royal Regiment of Horse (today The Blues and Royals), Lord Oxford. By now the army amounted to some 16,000 men. With the intention of overawing the metropolis, James instituted the garrison camp at Hounslow Heath to the west of London, a by-product of which was the creation of a special disciplinary court at Old Horse Guards. Judge Advocate General George Clarke describes its purpose:

> The army was encamped at Hounslow Heath where there were many courts martial at which I awaited, but a standing one was appointed to be held at Horse Guards every week with the General officers being President by turn. The intention of establishing this court was to withdraw the soldiery from the civil power, and all matters, civil as well as military, relating to the Army were to be brought before them.[128]

Inside Old Horse Guards the room used for these courts was the 'Great Room' over the archway, later called the Levee Room, and today the Major-General's suite.

Senior ministers and courtiers viewed with apprehension the implications of James's plans to make the army predominantly Catholic. Their alarm intensified on 10 June 1688, when the Prince of Wales was born at St James's Palace. A Roman Catholic monarchy was an unacceptable prospect, and opposition politicians opened secret negotiations with the Protestant courts of Europe. As a result, William of Orange, Stadtholder of the Netherlands was encouraged to invade England. When William and his army landed on the Devon coast on 5 November 1688, James gathered his army and marched to oppose them, but at Salisbury he changed his mind and returned to London. The army were divided in its loyalty, some escorting him back to the capital, some joining forces with William. Deprived of sufficient military support for his Catholic regime, James could not reign. Recognizing this, he accepted from William the assurance of a safe passage to France. On 17 December 1688, as William's Dutch Guards marched into Whitehall, a last show of resistance was offered by the Coldstream Guards on duty as the Tiltyard Guard. Their commanding officer, the octogenarian Lord Craven, stubbornly refused to dismount the guard until personally ordered to do so by James, stating, 'while breath remained in his body, no foreign force should make the King of England a prisoner in his own palace'.[129] The same evening James left for France to join his family. Sir George Arthur, historian of the Household Cavalry, thus summarized the situation: 'The Crown of England having been offered by a number of persons (who had no right to dispose of it) to two distinguished individuals (who equally had no right to accept it) the "Glorious Revolution" was complete.'[130] The new joint monarchs' Coronation took place on 23 February 1689, but archbishop of Canterbury, Thomas Tenison, refused 'on grounds of conscience' to officiate. His place was taken by the Bishop of London, Henry Compton, a former officer in the Blues, and of whom James once remarked that he spoke more like a colonel than a bishop!

'Alas, alas, Whitehall's consum'd to dust!'

After what was to be the last accession proclamation on 'the Green' on 13 February 1689, one of William's first acts was to ensure his Court was free of Catholic influences, especially in respect of the army. His Protestant Dutch 'Blue' Guards, under the command of Colonel Hendrik van Nassau Ouwerkerk and totalling 174 men, took over all Whitehall duties – at Horse Guards they mounted the King's Life Guard, initially on greys.[131] The three English Horse Guards troops were dispersed to Maidstone, Chelmsford and St Albans. The predominantly Roman Catholic fourth troop was disbanded, and the Royal Regiment of

The ruins of Whitehall Palace after the fire of 1698. This was the scene between the Thames and the highway for many months after the fire that consumed Whitehall Palace. A brief flurry of vast rebuilding schemes were publicized but none were seriously considered; instead, most of the burnt-out plots were leased to individuals for short-term lets, after which they reverted to the Crown. The forerunners of today's great public buildings then began to progressively appear along what was to become the Whitehall thoroughfare. The structures seen are the remains of Wolsey's Great Hall and the adjoining Chapel Royal. (Wren III:51, reproduced with permission of the Warden and Fellows of All Souls College, Oxford)

Horse was sent to Northampton for its duties. Finally, the new Roman Catholic chapel in the Privy Gallery was closed and its contents sold away.

Subsequently, William was to spend very little time at Whitehall, as the damp air aggravated his asthma. He preferred Kensington Palace, and as a consequence the number and responsibility of the Dutch guards at Old Horse Guards became reduced. Inevitably, lapses of security ensued as Paymaster's clerk Roger Syzer advised his master, the Earl of Ranelegh, 'Upon the arrival of the Dutch Troops and the removal of the English, the sentinels not placed as they used to be, five men broke into the Pay Office and took away an iron chest with £400.'[132]

On 10 April 1691, a serious fire consumed much of the newly rebuilt riverside range of apartments at Whitehall; Queen Mary and Princess Anne escaped on foot safely to Arlington House escorted by a Tiltyard Guard detachment after a 'sentinel gave the alarm by firing his musket'. The master gunner of Whitehall, ordnance engineer Captain Sylver at the Old Horse Guards armoury, used some of his powder barrels to blow a firebreak between the buildings, so successfully containing the fire.[133] The full extent of this 'suddaine and terible Fire'[134] can be seen to the lower left of Knyff's view of Whitehall, the blackened buildings depicting the burnt-out area. Plans for rebuilding were quickly drafted, but with William more or less permanently absent from the palace interest soon evaporated. However, as a token gesture, and to please the Queen (who loved Whitehall), the king did authorize the construction of a waterside patio for his wife. Built by Wren between 1691 and 1693, 'Queen Mary's Terras' was built along the embankment on the

site of the burnt-out Privy Stairs. With its four lawns clearly depicted by Knyff (p.57), part of the terrace still survives today in fragmentary form at the back of the Ministry of Defence, just off Horse Guards Avenue.

In 1697, following a reduction of hostilities on the Continent, Parliament voted to reduce the size of the army and also utilized this opportunity to return William's Dutch Guard to Holland. Thus, after a nine-year interval, the troops of English Horse Guards once again stood duty in their sentry boxes opposite the palace. As one contemporary source recorded, 'The Life Guards have returned home from Flanders, and have taken up again their peace duties at the Horse Guards.'[135] But the palace they guarded was about to vanish!

White-hall utterly burnt to the ground, nothing but the walls & ruines left!'[136]

With this bleak statement, John Evelyn records in his diary the sense of stunned shock that followed the news of the total devastation by fire of the palace of Whitehall. A letter to the Earl of Huntingdon from Dr Nathaniel Johnston dated 6 January 1698 provides more detail:

The fire at Whitehall continued vehemently burning till 7 o'clock yesterday morning, though parts were blown up above a dozen times, so that now there is nothing except some walls and chimneys of all that noble palace remaining, except the great gate [Court Gate] and the buildings upon it, the banqueting house and half of the covered passage to the guard chamber [for Yeoman of the Guard]. All the new buildings from the great gate that is next the cockpit to the stone gallery and waterside are consumed, viz. the chapel, council chamber, the treasury, the Queen's lodgings, the Secretary's office, and adjoining. Then the King's lodgings and all the new buildings, the guard chamber, chapel and all other buildings from the court where the King's statue is to the passage to the water and above 100 yards further in Scotland Yard to the waterside and a full third part of the range of buildings on the lower end of the first court of Scotland Yard, which is a most lamentable spectacle. Where exactly and how it began is as yet so variously reported that I know not which to believe. I could not pass for the mountains of rubbish into the stone gallery. I was told that at least the case of my Lord Portland's lodging was standing. All the parts from near the house my Lord of Lichfield lived in to the Horse Guards were yesterday covered with heaps of goods rescued from the flames. After a great number of the rabble had got in all gates were shut, and it's generally said they refused entrance to the servants of the insuring officer against the fire. It was some hours ere they got [fire] engines to play and was 8 o'clock ere they begun to use gunpowder to blow up. I hear many persons were slain but we shall not hear particulars in many days. One or more who were condoling the loss was replied to by some Dutch soldiers that it was but an old house and they need not be so much concerned for it.[137]

Other, more sympathetic, tributes were penned: 'it is a dismal sight to behold such a glorious, famous, and much renowned palace reduced to a heap of rubbish and ashes, which the day before might justly contend with any palace in the world for riches, nobility, honour and grandeur'.[138]

Fire had threatened the existence of the palace many times, but with the Court now resident between Kensington and St James's for long periods, the Whitehall staterooms were largely unused, with only a skeleton caretaker staff for much of the time. The overall loss cannot be calculated: irreplaceable court records and archives, works of art and furnishings – all accumulated at Whitehall over nearly three centuries of state occupation – were destroyed, not to mention what had been carried over from the prior centuries of York Place occupancy. As the previous correspondent went on to state,

> The Damage done by this fiery disaster is at present unaccountable, the loss must be very great, and might have been greater had not the officers of the Guards taken care to stop the numerous crowds from pressing forward into houses where goods were removing … above twelve persons perished, among whom were two grenadiers.[139]

As on previous occasions, plans to rebuild the palace on a vast scale were proposed, William even going so far as to declare publicly that 'he would rebuild it much finer than before',[140] but nothing was ever done. Many of the proposed plans still survive, however, namely at All Souls College, Oxford, and at Chatsworth House.[141]

Old Horse Guards escaped the inferno, the highway acting as a natural firebreak, but now there was no palace for it to guard. To maintain state administrative stability and continuity, William immediately decreed that the Court's official home would no longer be Whitehall but instead St James's Palace; to this day,

Cardinal Wolsey's wine cellar. Together with the Banqueting House, this is one of only two complete original surviving buildings from the palace of Whitehall. To save it during the Thameside 1950s developments involved a monumental engineering effort of bodily moving the entire 1,000-ton structure, a quarter of an inch at a time, downwards 18 feet, and then sideways to finally come to rest nine feet west of its original site. (Reproduced by permission of English Heritage. NMR)

St James's has remained the titular residence of English sovereignty. In so doing, he provided Old Horse Guards with an additional role: already a Household Troops' duty barracks and an emergent War Office, from now it would also be the only official entrance through the Park to the Court and Palace of St James's, in which role it continues to the present day. At the same time, the south end of the Horse Guards site relinquished its ancient role as a proclamation site. This tradition also moved to St James's Palace, the balcony of the Friary Court assuming the duty from the old 'Green' on state occasions.

From 1698 also an augmented detachment from the Tiltyard Guard commenced their sentry-go duty at the gates of the new royal court of St James's Palace, replacing the smaller guard which had been provided there from the Restoration for the Duke of York and other family members. The St James's Palace Guard continues to the present day. The Foot Guards' Buckingham Palace duty commenced from c.1837. The Foot Guards' Guard Mounting for their Palace Guards continued on Horse Guards Parade until Victorian times when much of their administration and associated drills gradually removed to the newly built Westminster Guards Barracks (later, Wellington Barracks) in nearby Birdcage Walk. Their Queen's Guard Mounting, however, continued at St James's Palace. A 'Tiltyard Guard' detachment continued, uninterrupted, to march each day into Horse Guards to undertake its protective role at the south end of the national military headquarters. Recalling these times, a Horse Guards Parade 'Guard Mounting' of the Foot Guards is today still re-enacted with full ceremony every May. Traditionally the officers' Slow March on this parade is said to be a test of their sobriety instituted in George II's reign.

As a building, Whitehall Palace is no more: its scorched foundations now lie many feet below the bustle of the modern highway. However, one can still see relics of the palace. Most obvious is the Banqueting House (it was converted to the Chapel Royal soon after the fire);[142] a wine cellar of Cardinal Wolsey's York Place survives under Horse Guards Avenue;[143] some of Queen Mary's riverside 'terras' remains by the river wall of the Ministry of Defence; interior fittings from James's Roman Catholic chapel are in St James's, Piccadilly and also the parish church of Burnham on Sea; in the Museum of London is a scale model of a large part of the palace based on the 1670 ground plan survey.[144] At Knole House in Kent survives probably the finest collection of Stuart furniture and furnishings in the country. Much of it came from Whitehall Palace, courtesy of Charles Sackville, 6th Earl of Dorset; while Lord Chamberlain, he sent back to Knole House any royal furniture the Court deemed unfashionable or unnecessary. On request, the Knole guides will show visitors the contemporary monogram 'WP' stamped on the underside of items from Whitehall Palace. A final relic, which must have been familiar viewing to many ladies of the Court, is a ceiling painting from Charles II's bedchamber. Painted by John Michael Wright and entitled *Ad Astrae*, it praises the good fortune of the King's escape from Cromwell in 1651. It is now housed in the Castle Museum, Nottingham.

THE UNRULY MIX OF MILITARY AND CIVILIAN AT HORSE GUARDS

Military life was tough in these times, but it became infinitely more hazardous whenever a soldier fell foul of the civil authorities. In 1695, the king learned that soldiers committed to prison were being subjected to extreme brutality. William took a personal interest in these matters:

by special commission [he] appointed twenty Field officers under the Presidency of the Duke of Shrewsbury to meet on Wednesdays and Saturdays every week in Horse Guards at Whitehall to hear and determine all complaints amongst any officers and soldiers of the land forces, and to redress same.[145]

The tribunal sat for the first of its hearings on 21 February 1695. Speaking at a later date about his work, the clerk John Mosse recalls that he 'was employed to write, in the business of the army and the War Office at the Great Chamber in the Horse Guards'.[146] The following gives some idea of the variety of complaints covered:

At a meeting of the chief officers of the army in the Great Chamber at Horse Guards in relation to the petition of Elizabeth Culliford on behalf of the orphans of Captain William Webster (Lt.Gen.Kirk's Regt) who lost his life at Philipstown, Ireland, a payment of £122-10-0 was made out of Army contingencies.[147]

The case concerning soldiers demanding subsistence of 7/- per week from another soldier, besides other necessaries, to be laid before the general Officers of the army at their meeting at Horse Guards.[148]

Re Customs Commissioners presentment covering some of their officers who have been beaten, abused and hindered from performing their office in visiting a

The ceiling panel from the Whitehall Palace bedroom of Charles II, glorifying the providence that assisted in Charles's escape via the oak, after the battle of Worcester, 1651. Perhaps the most evocative survival of the Restoration ownership of Whitehall Palace. (Courtesy Nottingham City Museums and Galleries: Nottingham Castle)

dogger [trawler] lately arrived from Holland, by some of H.M. Troop of Guards... My Lords desire to lay this matter before the General Officers sitting at the Horse Guards for further prevention of the occurrence.[149]

The Board of Commissioners of the Royal Hospital, Chelsea, came into being on 3 March 1697 and soon after was booking the Chapel room at Old Horse Guards for its disability and pension assessment hearings, thus creating a further incursion on room space at the already overcrowded, crumbling building.

Another consequence of William's absence from Whitehall was that St James's Park had become even more accessible to the public than in previous reigns. In a report to the king about 'encroachments and abuses in the park' the Earl of Bath, as Chief Ranger, stated his alarm that 'the now great number of gates and openings in the park wall belonged to private persons, most of them of the greatest rank and quality'. On the plus side, he was also able to report that the illegal alehouses and other public houses in the Park had been forbidden and suppressed 'except the Sutlers adjoining the court of guard under the command of the Earl of Rumney, colonel of the Guards'.[150] It is not surprising that the colonel, in receipt of a comfortable percentage of the income from the sutlers, would have a vested interest in the removal of any competition.

Sutlers (or purveyors) did very well for themselves in various service environments; they also travelled abroad with their units. Those attached to the Guards regiments were entrepreneurs in every sense; for instance, in the 1690s Thomas Morin not only served the Tiltyard Guard at Horse Guards as sutler, but also had the contract for soldiers stationed at Somerset House, the Savoy and Kensington.[151] He also benefited from a smart tax dodge, in that sutlers' premises housed within the environs of a military garrison were exempt from the Land Tax, newly imposed from 1692. A trial case was held in 1693 against 'the sutler's house at Whitehall', but the judgment went against the Commissioners for Taxes. The defence's case – that the Whitehall guard in which the sutler operated his business was an exempt garrison

– was upheld, the legal test being that it was 'erected for the security of the island'. This saved Morin an annual charge of some 4 shillings to the pound on his property, both in the Tiltyard and at the other garrisons he served. This case set a precedent that would cost the Tax Office considerably more when applied to all the national defence sites with sutlerages fulfilling the above criteria.[152] The sutler's premises fulfilled a role akin to the village corner shop, acting as a local intelligence gathering and dissemination centre. The following notice from a *London Gazette* of 1679 illustrates this function of the sutler: 'Stolen or strayed from Widow Johnson of Paddington the 21 of this instant October, a white gray gelding, 15 hands, with a shorn mane half way, bob-tailed, and a bare spot on the near hip upon the stifling place. Whoever gives notice at Mr. John Birds, Sutler at the Horse Guards shall be well Rewarded.'[153]

But other intelligence shared amid the swirling tobacco smoke of the sutler's parlour could be less welcome, as John France, 'coffee man in the Tiltyard', discovered. In 1707, he was hauled up to give evidence before a House of Lords select committee chaired by the bishop of Oxford and convened to look into 'Publication of Libels from Newsletters', as circulated around the coffee houses of the time. The minutes are too extensive to repeat here, but France escaped censure on the grounds of being unaware of the content of the large volume of newsletters passing through the Tiltyard Coffee House.[154] An earlier observer had complained that 'we have the Coffee-House tables continually spread with the noisome Excrements of diseased and laxative Scribblers!'[155] The revised Articles of War of 1742 (in force to 1859) attempted to effect a tighter control whereby sutlers could forfeit full value of 'all goods sold during divine service', while those staying open 'after 9pm or before Reveille [waking call] would be under pain of being Dismissed from all future Suttling'.[156]

Returning briefly to the Earl of Bath's report on St James's Park, it is interesting to note the mention of a guard house,

> opposite Hyde Park gate at the west of the Park is a range of buildings of nine small rooms ... which building is in the custody of Crosby the gate-keeper and is a public alehouse, but alleged to be for the conveniency of the Foot Guard who have a small guard house against the said keeper's buildings...

Possibly this 'small guard house' is the building referred to in a series of accounts entries from some years earlier: 'To building a new Foot Guard House at the upper end of St. James's Park ... £141-13-2$^{1}/_{4}$.'[157] If so, then it is of considerable interest that the account includes a payment of £2-18-2 to Robert Streater. He was the king's Serjeant Painter and a great favourite of Charles II. Also, as one of Wren's principal decorative artists, he had worked at all the royal palaces, and had enriched the interiors of at least 13 of Wren's churches in the City of London – his reredos for St Michael's, Cornhill, survives. Elsewhere he provided the magnificent surviving ceiling for the Sheldonian Theatre in Oxford, and an allegorical landscape of Boscobel and Whiteladies commemorating Charles II's escape after Worcester, now on display at Hampton Court. At present, it is not known exactly what he provided for the Tiltyard Foot Guards' house in St James's Park: perhaps a miniature marvel of a ceiling piece that might come to light in the records at some future date?

Demise by decay: the decline of Old Horse Guards

ST JAMES'S PARK: 'THAT AMOUROUS SHADE'

Despite previous regulations, by the accession of Queen Anne (r.1702–14) the St James's Park and Green Park locality had become an established focus for gatherings and assignations. Each social fraternity occupied its accustomed one of the 20 or so 'walks' that criss-crossed the parks, such as 'The Green Walk', 'Duke Humphrey's Walk', 'The Close Walk', 'The Long Lime Walk' and 'The Jacobite Walk'. In Anne's view, however, the park was an integral part of the new St James's Court, and certain standards of respect and decorum within its environs had to be maintained. Consequently, in the spring of 1703, she issued some strict edicts to control what she viewed as the raffish and rowdy elements of London society that plagued 'her' Park. The implementation of these rules was the responsibility of the Tiltyard Guard, whose sentries were stationed around the Park precincts in various 'centinel boxes'. In brief, the rules were as follows: no person to ride on horseback; no coaches and carts permitted except the royal family's coach; no rude, disorderly persons or beggars allowed; no one permitted to sell anything there; hogs and dogs to be kept out; sentinels and gatekeepers to be stationed at every public gate; and no one to disturb the deer or wildfowl, or colts and fillies.

Many of these measures were to prove unenforceable; nevertheless, the rules also stated that the officer on guard send a corporal and soldiers when necessary to assist the keepers in their enforcement and bring the offenders before a Justice of the Peace. Today, one element of these statutes persists in that commercial vehicles are restricted in their use of the roads through St James's Park.

The Park was, of course, used for state occasions. At midday on 3 January 1705, the duty detachments of the Guards at Horse Guards were assembled on the parade ground to honour the procession of the Standards and Colours taken at the battle of Blenheim. The cavalcade marched through St James's Park to Westminster Hall. Also watching the parade was William Nicolson, future bishop of Carlisle, who described the colourful scene:

At 12 I went into the Park, to meet the Triumph; which passed that way about two. The Horse Guards, with Trumpets and Kettle-Drums, marched first; in the middle whereof were 32 Standards borne by so many Cornets with green feathers. The Troopers that led them had red Feathers, and the followers white. After a Company or two of Fusiliers, came 128 Colours; some of which were torn to the very Staff. These were followed by the rest of the Foot-Guards; the whole cavalcade being near an hour in passing by.[158]

According to Household Cavalry historian Sir George Arthur, the procession was led by the Horse Grenadier Guards, the Standards were carried by Life Guardsmen, and the 128 Colours borne by 'pikemen' of the Foot Guards.[159]

But St James's Park also observed the harsh public face of military life, as noted in a 1727 newsletter: 'A private Centinel in the Guards, having been detected in frequenting Popish Conventicles, was whipped on the Parade in St. James's Park by about 300 Men, receiving 3 lashes from each Centinel, and was after drummed out of the Regiment with the usual marks of Ignominy.'[160] This report contains possibly the earliest mention of the Parade Ground as a specific location in its own right within St James's Park and associated with Guards' regimental events.

REPAIRS AND RENOVATIONS

In November 1703, one of the worst storms in England's history occurred, destroying property on a huge scale, including the Eddystone lighthouse, and killing thousands. Also, said Daniel Defoe, 'the Roof the Guard-House at Whitehall was quite blown off ... nine souldiers were hurt, but none of them died'.[161]

The already inherently rickety structure of the building was further weakened by the effects of the

A view from St James's Park of Old Horse Guards showing its adjoining mix of Tudor, Jacobean, Carolean and Georgian architecture. Note the Old Horse Guards clock with its one-hand dial; it struck the hours only, on a single bell. To its left is the first Admiralty of 1694–95, then to its right the Banqueting House, the Holbein Gate, the Great Close turreted tennis court of Henry VIII, next the first Treasury building, with extreme right, the Earl of Lichfield's house, later to become famous as 10 Downing Street. (J. Kip, Guildhall Library, City of London)

storm. Over the next two decades, the commanding officers of the Guards regiments at Old Horse Guards, both cavalry and foot, were to engage a reluctant Treasury in a running battle for funding to prevent the entire building from collapsing.

The last years of Anne's reign and the early years of George I (r.1714–27) are characterized by Parliament's increasing strictures on military expenditure. No distinction was made between army executive and field units: all suffered equally from the Treasury's mandates of thrift – a response to the costs of financing the wars on the Continent. At Old Horse Guards, requests and estimates for urgent structural repairs were delayed, ignored or pared to an absolute minimum. Tradesmen became increasingly wary of taking on military contracts as all bills were years being settled and many not at all. As early as January 1704, payments to workmen for 'Repaires done at ye Horse Guards' were outstanding to the value of £895-8-8.[162] Three years later, this increased by another £217-9-0 for works to the 'Officers Roomes', the 'Little Guardhouse', the 'Great Guardhouse', the 'Sutlers and the Major's house'. The 'Little Guardhouse' was, of course, the Tiltyard Guard. These repairs did eventually get done but only because the estimate was endorsed by Sir Christopher Wren as 'absolutely necessary'.[163]

By August 1710, further deterioration had occurred, as described by Major-General Richard Holmes of the Coldstream Guards:

the Guard roomes at the Tilt Yard are so exceedingly out of repair that neither the Officers nor Soldiers can lay dry upon Guard, insomuch that the Bedding and Furniture are almost quite rotten and not only the furniture but even the wainscott is almost decayed and except Speedy Care be taken, the Guard roomes are in danger of falling...[164]

The Treasury took until November to produce an estimate of £454-10-11, the repairs not being effected until the following year. Both the War Office departments at Old Horse Guards and the Chelsea Board of Commissioners took the decision at this time to vacate the building, preferring safer and more hygienic premises nearby. The former crossed the road to 7 Whitehall, while from 1712 the latter met at an office in Killigrew Street, Middle Scotland Yard. In 1713 the patience of the long-suffering Household troops came to an end. Forced to carry out their guard duties in reduced numbers due to insufficient living quarters in a structurally dangerous and unsanitary building, their commanding officers requested an official investigation into the crisis. In February 1713, Lord Treasurer William Lowndes ordered Wren to prepare a report on the situation.

Although by now an old man of 81, Wren submitted a detailed survey in March saying that from the original design for 108 horses, the building could now only house 62. He went on to detail the missing 46 spaces as '11 horses taken by the Sutler at the south end ... additional to his Convenient House Built when the Stables were Built'. The Paymaster's encroachment at the north-west corner had removed spaces for 30 horses, while on the west side stables for five horses had been taken out for the Judge Advocate. He concluded his report with the comment, 'How these Encroachments may be recovered, We humbly leave to

Your Lordship's Great Wisdom.'[165] Their Lordships never came up with an answer, and the 'encroacht' stabling space was lost for good to the Horse Guards. In fact, the stabling could only accommodate 50 horses as of September 1714.[166]

By September 1717, the decay of Guard quarters at all the London palaces had become endemic. The following summary was submitted to the Treasury as a minimum requirement for buildings that were 'in a very ruinous condition ... almost ready to fall': Kensington £161-17-6; St James's £288-00-1; Tilt Yard £486-2-2; Whitehall [Horse Guards] £367-6-2; a rebuild of Whitehall Sutler's house £800-00-0; Incidentals £96-14-1, in all a total of £2,200-00-0. Receiving this estimate at Treasury Chambers Secretary Charles Stanhope blanched at the mountainous cost and rushed out the response that 'their Lordships Can by no means advise so great

an Expense to the Publique!' The Guards replied, 'we cannot undertake that the same shall be executed at a lesser expence than before mentioned', but in conciliation, 'the Sutler's house could be secured for the present by Shores and Buttresses ... but the uncertainty of Estimating of workes of this Nature arises from the difficulty of seeing into the Defects of old Crazy Buildings...'[167] The Treasury was left with little choice but to authorize the expense; however, soon after the responsibility for repairs to Guard Houses was transferred to the Board of Ordnance, which itself was strictly instructed by the Duke of Marlborough 'to use the utmost frugality therein'.[168]

The principal contributor to these delays was the confused system of military responsibility that resulted from the mix of civil and military officialdom at Old Horse Guards. From his temporary office across the road, Secretary-at-War Henry St John was the

An unfinished view of Old Horse Guards from the Park of about 1749. The detail displayed clearly shows the ad hoc chimney stacks thrust through roofs not originally designed to accept them. A consequence of the endless fight for working space in the rooms below. (P. Sandby, Guildhall Library, City of London)

principal civil administrator of the army. His was the approval sought for establishments of regiments, rates of pay and allowances, and his was the final decision on arbitration between conflicting civil and military interests. Subordinate to the Secretary-at-War were the military Adjutant General and the Quartermaster General (QMG). The former attended to returns, duty rosters, orders, general discipline and, through the Ordnance Board, the issue of arms. The QMG's department was smaller and looked after the general provisioning and movement logistics of the army. Somewhere between these officers in seniority, the controllers of army accounts exercised financial control of the affairs of Old Horse Guards in its role as Commander-in-Chief's office.

From 1720 to 1744 there was no appointed Commander-in-Chief, so management of the army at home and abroad devolved solely upon the Secretary-at-War. Lord Stair was eventually appointed C-in-C on 24 February 1744; however, in the following year the muddled administration of George II also appointed Marshal Wade as C-in-C and, on the same date, the Duke of Cumberland as Captain General of the Forces. With Stair's commission running from February 1744 to June 1746, Wade's from March 1745 to December 1745, and Cumberland's from March 1746 to October 1757, the British forces fell under the command of three separate Commanders-in-Chief at the same time. Small wonder that no effective action was forthcoming to keep Old Horse Guards from falling down.

Meanwhile, around the crumbling structure of Old Horse Guards, new buildings were erected on the burnt-out sites of the old palace – the forerunners of the great government office blocks of present-day Whitehall. The old Tiltyard Gallery and its adjoining Park Stairs were demolished in 1716. In their place a new house was built by Viscount Falmouth, Comptroller of the Royal Household. This later became Dover House. A significant Household Cavalry occupant of Dover House was Jeffrey, Lord Amherst. A lifetime soldier, Amherst successively held the colonelcies of the 2nd Horse Grenadier Guards, and the 2nd Life Guards Regiment. Later, he was C-in-C 1778–82 and 1793–95. But his career was destined always to be historically blighted by his being the senior military commander in office at the time the American colonies were lost to Washington and his dedicated followers.

In 1723, to widen the now extremely busy Whitehall thoroughfare, the Cromwellian gun battery alongside the Holbein Gate was dismantled and the adjoining Privy Garden wall set back to its pre-1533 line. Since the 1698 fire the original palace Privy Garden had become a public area of grassland mostly walled off from the street; it continued, however, to be guarded for public order purposes by two sentries from the Tiltyard Guard.[169] In 1726, the first Admiralty to the north of Horse Guards was replaced by today's much larger building by Thomas Ripley. A further feature during this era of Whitehall's enhancement was the restoration in 1729 of the Rubens ceiling in the Banqueting House, which had been damaged in the fire. This delicate task was entrusted to a man destined to be intimately associated with Horse Guards, the gifted architect William Kent.[170] As deputy Surveyor General and Commissioner to the Board of Works, Kent was about to embark upon a series of commissions to change the face of much of Whitehall.

New Horse Guards

Italy comes to Whitehall

William Kent's popularity as an architect stemmed from his revival, sponsored by Lord Burlington, of the classical architectural themes of the Italian Andrea Palladio, first used in England by the Inigo Jones/John Webb partnership a century earlier. In 1727, Kent had published a collection of designs from Palladio, originally edited by Jones, which were seen as a fresh and sophisticated alternative to the now rather hackneyed baroque school.[171]

Continuing his assault on the Tudor and Stuart relics of Whitehall, Kent in 1732 rebuilt the Royal Mews, this was sited where the National Gallery now is. In 1683 it had been adapted to house the Horse Grenadiers: they were stabled there in Kent's new building until 1788. Also came the new Treasury building (1733–36), just south of Horse Guards, on the site of Henry VIII's Cockpit, and still there today. Its upper rooms afforded the Treasury clerks a fine panoramic view of St James's Park; however, there were disadvantages, as Treasury minister J. Scrope complained to Secretary-at-War Sir William Strickland:

> The exercising of soldiers which is almost every day now done before the Treasury at Whitehall in the morning when the Treasury Lords are sitting, and with drums beating, gives great disturbance to the business of the

office. It is therefore their Lordship's desire that the said exercise with drums be performed in some other place.[172]

The comments of the Guards' commanding officers on being informed of 'their Lordship's desire' can be imagined, taking into account the same Treasury Lordships' spending record (or lack of it) on behalf of the Guards over the past half century or so.

In 1732, the Treasury looked after its own, authorizing the complete rebuilding of the northern wing of Old Horse Guards as a separate, self-contained building to house the Paymaster General, the Commissary General, and the commissioners of the Chelsea Royal Hospital. Also included was a grace and favour residence for the Paymaster on the ground floor. As token compensation for the further stabling lost to the Horse Guards, about half a dozen stalls were left squeezed into the ground floor. Built by John Lane, costing £3,842-10-11 and finally completed in 1733, the Paymaster's Office survived largely unaltered to the late 1950s.[173]

Kent's new Treasury had been completed the previous year. In its accounts is to be found a comment further confirming the existence of the Parade Ground as a now established part of St James's Park:

That by the frequent passage of Carts, laden with Stone and other heavy Materials during the Rebuilding the Office of his Majs. Treasury, the Opening in St. James's Park called the Parade has been very much worn and Rendered almost impassable. That as the said Building is now so far Completed as no longer to require passage for Materials of those heavy kinds it may be a proper time to Repair the said Parade, to restore the Park to its Beauty and Convenience.[174]

At this date it had yet to become 'Horse Guards' Parade. The earliest source known at present where it is so recorded is the diary of Regency gentleman, Joseph Farington. On Saturday, 2 August 1817, he writes, 'At 10 called on Mr. C. Long but He being dressing I went to the Horse Guards parade and saw the Guard relieved. At 1/2 past 10 I returned to Mr. Long...'[175] That the ceremony Mr. Farington watched took about half an hour perhaps indicates it was a Household Cavalry guard change. Had it been a Foot Guards 'Tiltyard Guard' ceremony, involving as this did the best part of a hundred men, it could have taken some time longer. It is interesting to note that by this time the regular event had moved imperceptibly from being just a formal military drill parade to an established public spectacle that people went out of their way to watch.

However, the Horse Guards locality was one to avoid after dark, especially following the Gin Riots. In September 1736, Bow Street magistrate Colonel De Veil was in continuous contact with the Tiltyard and the Horse Guards, waiting for any 'Disturbances' to happen. In fact, the Horse Guards' guard was reinforced 'in order to suppress any Tumult that might happen at the going down of Spirituous Liquors'.[176] None of this, however, was sufficient to prevent the following altercation, as recorded in a contemporary source:

At one in the morning a Captain Wilson and a Captain Skerrett of Ffoulkes Regiment, having quarrelled in

OPPOSITE
William Kent, architect of the present Horse Guards. The leading classical architect of his day, Kent, assisted by John Vardy, successfully submitted rebuilding plans to replace Old Horse Guards in 1747. However, he died in April 1748, and Vardy then completed the rebuilding to Kent's largely unaltered design over the next decade. (Bartholomew Dandridge, National Portrait Gallery, London)

the Street at Whitehall, were separated by the sentries, Captain Wilson being wounded in the cheek. On coming into the Tiltyard Coffee House they drew again and Captain Wilson received another wound in the shoulder but ran through Captain Skerrett who died immediately. Wilson made his escape; manslaughter was the Coroner's verdict as the deceased was adjudged the aggressor.[177]

Perhaps the 'open all hours' Tiltyard Coffee House was a contributory factor.

Between 1746 and 1755 the Italian artistic genius Canaletto lived in London. It is uniquely fortunate that, while here, he chose to depict both the Old Horse Guards and the New Horse Guards buildings in several paintings. Viewed in a vista of 'Venetian' sunlight from St James's Park, he gives Old Horse Guards a perfection of detail that it certainly lacked at that date (c.1748), with its rickety, collapsing brickwork. Canaletto created his final works from his detailed sketches and notes (as opposed to painting the works on site); hence the artistic license. For New Horse Guards, he shows the north block completed, and the central block and clock tower complete but lacking the clock for which scaffolding is in place. The south wing is shown as not started.[178] Even given his artistic licence, Canaletto provides by far the most detailed representation of the Horse Guards frontages to the Park, though he had left London before New Horse Guards was complete: it is regrettable only that he never had time to depict either subject from Whitehall.

It is possible, nevertheless, that Canaletto may have unwittingly recorded the earliest known depiction of the ceremony at Horse Guards that we know today as 'Trooping the Colour'. His painting *Old Horse Guards from St James's Park* has been dated as c.1748. It certainly shows the building as an active military garrison – its demolition commenced in early 1750. The complete Tiltyard Guard, totalling possibly 100 all ranks, is seen on Guard Mounting parade with the Colour at its centre. The earliest surviving written orders describing such parades, with the Colour being trooped and lodged with attendant courtesies and procedures, are dated February 1749 in First Guards (i.e. Grenadier) and Coldstream Guards Order Books.[179] Does this particular view by Canaletto depict an enactment of these orders – a 'Trooping' – in 1748?

In his *Critical Review of the Buildings of London* (1734) James Ralph wrote, 'I can't help wishing that the station of the Horse Guards, and the adjoining military apartments, were pulled down, and others in a more consistent and regular taste erected in their room.' A decade or so later his wish neared reality as two senior Life Guard officers led a representation to the highest levels that Old Horse Guards was now completely uninhabitable. Gold Stick-in-Waiting Lord de la Warr, together with Lord Cadogan and Judge Advocate General Thomas Morgan submitted the following memorial to Secretary-at-War Sir William Yonge on 3 May 1745:

The whole building belonging to the Horse Guards being in a very rotten and decayed condition and having been supported many years by props in the stable, the whole weight of the building lying thereon it is now become so dangerous that it is not safe for the coaches of His Majesty and the Royal Family to pass under the gateway, and the men and horses doing duty there are in perpetual danger of losing their lives by the falling down of the building especially in stormy weather, and the stacks of the chimneys are grown so bad that though constantly kept swept are subject to take fire. The expense of supporting this ruinous building is daily increasing, so that money laid out upon it is entirely thrown away.[180]

The memorial was referred to the Treasury which, on 4 July, ordered the Board of Works to further shore up the brickwork and to 'prepare plans for rebuilding'.[181] The cost of shoring up was £160, and then the Board, consisting of Henry Finch, surveyor, Thomas Ripley

comptroller, William Kent, architect, and his assistants John Vardy and Westby Gill, set about producing plans for a new Horse Guards building. Clearly, considering the acceptance of his previous work in Whitehall, the ideas of William Kent were bound to dictate the final form the new building would take.

It was in art rather than architecture that Yorkshireman William Kent first prospered, his exceptional skill for decorative design recognized when he was still an apprentice coach painter. Sir William Wentworth sponsored him on a tour through Italy to study painting and, in exchange, Kent purchased statues and other *objets d'art* for Sir William's home. That the tour was profitable is evident from Kent being the first Englishman to be admitted to

Old Horse Guards in Canaletto's sketchbook, 1749. The artist's preparatory notes for the illustration on page 78 reveal how closely he studied his subject, but in the finished work (completed in his studio) he allowed distance to lend its enchantment to this view of a very rickety building. The letters used on his sketch are C = copi (tiles), B = bianco (light), R = rosso (brick), P = piombo (lead). (Museo Accademia, Venice)

two London works – a royal palace in Hyde Park and a new Houses of Parliament – although approved in design, were never put into effect. The national debt aftermath from the European wars made such projects courtly pipe-dreams. The Kent/Burlington partnership's greatest surviving work is Holkham Hall, designed for the Earl of Leicester, whom Kent had also met on his Italian tour. Kent's versatility as a designer extended beyond architecture into landscape gardening – at Rousham, Oxford, for Lieutenant General James Dormer; and to boat building – a royal barge for the Prince of Wales.

Although Kent was to die in 1748, just before the reconstruction of Horse Guards finally got under way, his long-time friend and assistant on the Board of Works, John Vardy, ensured that the original designs prepared by Kent were carried into effect with as little alteration as possible.

The demolition of Old Horse Guards almost occurred prematurely with an accidental fire in April 1747:

Old Horse Guards, 1749. Canaletto's almost photographic perfection of detail is illusory here: the accounts' entries for this date detail the building's brickwork as disjointed and in danger of complete collapse. For instance the balcony, originally overhanging the main door, has by this date fallen off the building. Under the trees at the extreme left can be discerned one of the many sentry boxes scattered around St James's Park for use by sentries of the Tiltyard Guard. (© Christie's Images Limited)

the Grand Duke of Tuscany's Academy of Art. Also touring Italy at the time was the Earl of Burlington. He and Kent struck up a professional friendship that prospered immediately after their return to England together in 1719. The earl saw William Kent as the ideal person to promote and put into practice his favourite designs of the Italian renaissance architect Andrea Palladio, while Kent saw in the earl a source of many fruitful commissions, initially in decoration and later in architecture. The partnership was to be very successful, with Kent called upon by many of the nobility to enrich the interiors of their country houses, and Burlington's influence at court securing for Kent the post of architect to the Board of Works. Thus he was allowed the opportunity to design Palladian-style large-scale public buildings, such as the Treasury, the Royal Mews, and the New Horse Guards. Kent's other

the coffee room and part of the sutling house at the Tiltyard was blown up by an accidental explosion of gun-powder in an under-room. Four or five soldiers in the coffee rooms were burnt and sent to hospital, others jumped out of the window, some passers-by were hurt but the fire did not spread.[182]

A further interim report made on 15 July 1749 by architect Joseph Pratt and Clerk of Works John Vardy to Surveyor General Henry Finch highlighted the extreme danger that the fabric of Old Horse Guards presented:

Old Horse Guards from St James's Park, c.1748. Here Canaletto views his subject from the south-west. The Parade Ground area has by now assumed some two-thirds of its present-day dimensions; this view shows it merging into the grassland of the park of which, of course, the Parade has always been a constituent part. In the left background is seen a residual length of the Tudor brick wall with which Henry VIII originally entirely enclosed what was his private hunting park. The Tiltyard Guard parading appears to total at least 80 men, assuming their Colour is at the centre of the line and that Canaletto accurately represented their number. The actual total is probably closer to 100 given the Guard patrolled all of what is today St James's and Green Park, the royal Privy Garden (then behind the Banqueting Hall), and the security of the public access road through the palace down to the Thameside public landing stage. (Guildhall Library, City of London)

We have this day view'd ... and Search'd into the present State ... of ... the Horse Guards ... at Whitehall. With Regard to the said Building in Generall the Decay is so Obvious on the Externall Appearance, that it wants no Discription to Shew its Weakness, Yet Upon a Mature Consideration We find such defects that in Our humble opinion it ought immediately to be Secur'd, particularly the middle part or high Building, the North and South end of which being of Brick is built on Girders quite across the Stables, which from the great weight has given way and entirely disjointed the said Brickwork. And as there is a Cupola in the Center of the said Building, the Principall Timbers of which under the flatt are rolled, and as the said Timbers are not Shored or secur'd above the said Flatt, we apprehend the Cupola being about Thirty feet high above the said Flatt is in Great Danger. And we think it absolutley necessary (for present safety) to put proper Supports under the Gateway next St. James's Park, and in such other places as will more particularly appear from the Plans of the said Building as will be laid before your honours...[183]

But Old Horse Guards was to hover on the verge of total collapse for more than another year before the final plans and estimates for a total rebuild were laid before the Treasury for approval, the Board of Works submitting the following memorial on 5 September 1749:

In the Principal or Middle Building there may be a room for the holding of Courts Martial, a Chapel, and an Office for the Secretary-at-War, as well as an apartment for the Judge Advocate General, and likewise a Board Room and other conveniences for the Commissioners of

General's office and likewise proper conveniences for the Horse Officers, and for Corn, Hay, and Straw necessary for ye stables. As this will be a public building and fronts the one way to the King's Park, and the other way to the great passage leading to the Houses of Parliament, we propose it to be built in a very substantial manner, and the whole faced with Portland stone. We beg leave to observe to your Lordships that this building may be completely finished in four years time, that the Middle part and buildings on the north side may be first built so that the Foot Guards may be placed over the new stables and the officers may be in the Middle Building until the building on the south side for the Foot Guards is completed. We estimate the cost to be £7937 per annum – in all £31748.[184]

With no accommodation earmarked for a Commander-in-Chief, from the outset the new Horse Guards building was clearly intended to operate as a civil office primarily concerned with the ministerial government of the army. Its importance as a guard headquarters for the Horse Guard troops and Foot Guards was significantly lessened, as evidenced from the meagre stabling provided and the almost afterthought comment in the proposal document 'with two rooms for the Officers of the Horse Guards'.

the Chelsea Hospital, with two rooms for the Officers of the Horse Guards. On the south side of the Middle Building and court is proposed a Guardroom, and rooms for the Officers of the Foot Guards, larger and better than they now are, and a Sutling House, with other proper conveniences. On the north side of the Middle Building and court is designed stabling for sixty two horses, exclusive of the stable now under the Paymaster

While final Treasury approval was awaited, the Secretary-at-War, Henry Fox, made temporary arrangements for 'good and sufficient stabling for fifty eight horses ... on a certain piece of ground on the west side of James Street in the parish of St. Margaret',[185] today Buckingham Gate. By March 1750, the Horse Guards Troops had removed to James Street, but it was not until 24 April that final royal approval was received 'to proceed in pulling down and rebuilding the Horse Guards with all expedition agreeable to their plan, taking care to use as little of the Park as possible'.[186]

Some of the occupants of the old building were allowed to remove items they wished to incorporate into the new one. This included the Foot Guards' sutler John Fry who, amongst other things, took one item described as a 'Frontis Piece next the Street'. This seems most probably to have been a sign mounted somewhere on the Whitehall external wall of the Old Horse Guards building advertising the Tiltyard Coffee House to the passing public. Whether it was later fixed to the exterior of the new building is not known. Further sutlery detail in the same document reveals the existence of a 'lower Tap Room', a 'Cellar', a 'Tap Room' and an 'Upper Tap Room', all of which tends to confirm that the business took up three floors in the south-east wing.[187]

A temporary passageway into the Park was made across the north of the site. The first stones of the central block of today's building were laid during August 1750; by June 1753 this had been completed, together with the northern wing. However, the cost at that date from the three books of John Calcraft's 'settled accompts' is revealed as £31,063-13-11³/₄d, wildly out of line with the original estimate for the whole project of £31,748. His next books for March 1754 to March 1757 show an expenditure of £25,100, while the final period March 1757 to June 1760 amounted to £8,900. The books for June 1753 to March 1754 are missing, so an exact final figure remains unknown; nevertheless, the recorded expenditure of some £65,000 shows the extent of the Board's underestimation. Calcraft was appointed by the Treasury as project paymaster, and his contract allowed him to retain a 5 per cent charge levied on all trader's bills 'to pay fees of office'.[188] Thus, by 1760 he had made himself at least £3,250.[189]

The new Horse Guards was a very high-profile project, so much so that the Board members were to

Elevation of New Horse Guards. This engraving by John Vardy shows Kent's original classical Palladian 'country house' conception, with the wings attached to the centre block by a low storey. However, by the 1800s the incessant pressure for more office space saw further storeys added between the wings, giving the building its present appearance. (J. Vardy, Guildhall Library, City of London)

Did Horse Guards ever look like this? This 1752 engraving by J. Maurer is accompanied by his 1754 version showing the building complete with tower. However, the rebuilding minutes clearly record that the north wing and central block and tower of the building were virtually complete before the Foot Guards' south wing was started. On 1 February 1753 is recorded, 'Mr. Andrew Jelfe attended and received the Board's directions for putting into execution the Dome on which the Turret is to stand.' By 3 April the tower was ready to receive the clock, 'Order'd that the Opening of the clock Dial Plate be made larger and the figures a small matter shorter.' Six weeks later the rebuilt clock was installed. The south wing was started on 7 June 1754: 'Gave directions for digging out the Foundations of the new building for the Foot Guards.' Finally, Canaletto's view clearly shows the north wing and tower complete, with the clock scaffolding in situ, *but the south wing not yet started. Perhaps Maurer was sympathetic with Hogarth and (continued)*

meet on 181 occasions during the eventual ten years of construction. Their minute books read almost like a diary; to study them is to sit at the desks of Surveyor General Henry Finch, Clerk of Works John Vardy, and architectural draughtsman Isaac Ware as they narrate the technical, financial and political problems encountered at each stage of construction. Without question, the Board is revealed as a team of highly skilled and dedicated men to whose conscientiousness and artistry the Horse Guards building remains a lasting memorial.

The actual building records for the new Horse Guards are voluminous; any interested reader is directed to the Public Record Office where the surviving ministerial Office of Works documents can be studied. Additionally, preserved in the library of the Royal Institute of British Architects are four volumes of ledger accounts (with some gaps) for the on-site work between 1750 and 1760, detailing each artisan's contribution.[190]

By 1760, the rebuilding of Horse Guards was complete. As one approaches the Parade Ground through the trees of St James's Park today, the panoramic view of its imposing façade is irresistibly attractive; when newly built the view must have been even more striking. William Kent's Palladian 'country house' design for Horse Guards has aroused architectural comment, informed or otherwise, ever since. He took the basic principle of Palladio's designs – a large central block containing the main living apartments flanked by symmetrical rectangular wings housing service rooms – and, within the extremely confined area of the Horse Guards site, developed the proportions vertically, resulting in a composition of box-like pavilions and turrets of varying heights and sizes. The space previously taken by the northern wing of Old Horse Guards for the Paymaster, a frontage of some 50 feet, was lost to John Lane's new Paymaster General's building. Furthermore, the development of Dover House in 1721 had taken another 25 feet off the south end of the site, leaving Kent little option but to extend his building upwards in order to find the requisite office space.[191] Contemporary criticisms were aimed mainly at the fact that the building, in particular its archway, looked far too ignoble for its royal role as the official entrance to the Court of St James's.

William Hogarth, avowed enemy of the Burlington school, ridiculed it mercilessly in picture and verse.[192] But let Margaret Jourdain, biographer of William Kent, provide an apt final comment: 'The architect of the Horse Guards, of the fragment of the Treasury, of Holkham ... must, if his great unexecuted projects are taken into consideration as well, be recognized as the most considerable figure of the Palladian movement.'[193]

By 1758, the Horse Guards Troops and the Foot Guards (the Coldstreams were first on 14 May 1756) had all moved back into their new quarters at Horse Guards to continue their guard duties while the Board of Works finished the structural detailing. One specific point of the latter involved the clock surmounting the building. As noted earlier, the Old Horse Guards clock was by Thomas Herbert; his mechanism was so accurate in performance that it gave Old Horse Guards' clock a reputation

(continued) the anti-Kent/Burlington school and so indulged himself with this capriccio vision. (Maurer, Courtesy of the Council, National Army Museum)

Canaletto's confirmation of the comments about Maurer's view. This shows the north wing completed, the scaffolding in place for the clock's installation in the completed central tower section, and the south (Foot Guards) wing not yet started. (© Christie's Images Limited)

Maurer's 1754 version of Horse Guards as completed. Like the p.82 illustration, his conception is open to question. The date must be 1756 or later, given the finished south wing, in use May 1756. In fact, this could be the same procession as shown by Boydell opposite, namely the King's first official use of his new processional gateway. (J. Maurer, Guildhall Library, City of London)

similar to that currently enjoyed by Big Ben. Many contemporary rhyming couplets attest to its fame, one such by Thomas Moore being,

'Six by the Horse Guards!
Old Georgy is late – But come, lay the table cloth – zounds, do not wait!'

On 28 November 1752, some 90 years on from Herbert's work, the initial step towards a more modern clock was taken when the rebuild board, 'Order'd Mr. Davis Clockmaker examine the State and Condition the Old Clock is in that belongs to the Horse Guards'.[194]

This was John Davis (1690–1762) who appears in the Court registers as 'Clockmaker to King George II'. On 5 December, he made the following report to the Board:

the Old Clock belonging the Horse Guards is in a very bad condition, but if it were the Board's pleasure to have it put into thorough repair, And an additional Work made to direct a Minute hand; that might be done for about £60. And if it were requir'd to Strike the quarters and to have Minute hands, that in that case the Clock must be Intirly new, and cannot be performed for less than the Sum of £140-00-0. And an extra Bell which may Cost about £14-00-0.[195]

It is interesting that Davis details an 'extra' bell, so implying that one was already hung in the new building, and the 'extra' being for the proposed quarter striking option: possibly the *in situ* one was the original from the Old Horse Guards.

The Board retired to think economies over the Christmas period and then, on 1 February, recorded that 'Mr. Seddon Clockmaker waited on the Board desiring he might be Indulg'd in Making the Necessary repairs to the Horse Guards Clock, as that his Father and Him has had the Care of the said Clock for upwards of Sixty years, and have always receive'd a Sallery for their said care.' The Board then 'Order'd that Mr. Seddon do make an Estimate of what will be the Charge of Putting the said Clock into a good and Substantial Repair, And likewise for makeing an aditional new Work to carry two Minutes hand One to the Dyal Plate and the other to the West.' On 8 May, 'Mr. Seddon attended and Acquainted the Board that he shall have completed the Repairs and Additional works to the Clock in six weeks time.' Seddon, a St James's watchmaker, submitted an

A state procession passing through the new Horse Guards, c.1758. The Holbein Gate dominating the centre was demolished in 1759, and the south wing of Horse Guards was not completed until 1756. At the bottom right of the Holbein Gate can just be glimpsed a small square-topped doorway set in a few feet of wall: this is the remaining public entrance to the Tiltyard Sutling/Coffee House complex. (J. Boydell, Guildhall Library, City of London)

William Hogarth ridicules Horse Guards. In this acid satire from his Canvassing for Votes *engraving (1757) Hogarth, who detested the Kent/Burlington school of architecture, depicts on the inn sign a royal coachman being decapitated by the apparent inadequate height of Horse Guards arch. He added to his criticism the following lines of invective: 'There see the Pile, in modern Taste, On top with tub-like Turret grac'd: Where the cramp'd Entrance, like some Shed, Knocks off the Royal Driver's Head. Lives there a Wit but what will cry "An Arch so low is mighty high!"' (W. Hogarth, by courtesy of the Trustees of Sir John Soane's Museum)*

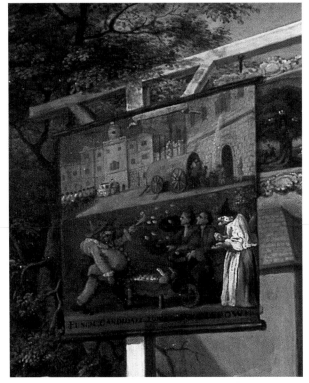

eventual bill for £52-12-6 'for putting into good and substantial repair the Present Clock ... and adding to the Said clock an intire new Dial Work to carry two Minute hands'.[196]

But the Board's pursuance of economy was to prove false, because the clock that today tells the time to Whitehall was installed in 1768 by London's oldest clockmakers, Thwaites & Reed, to replace Seddon's make do and mend. When this new clock had its first major overhaul in 1789, the opportunity was taken to provide a new chime, including the tuneful 'ting-tang' quarter-striking bells, from London's oldest bell foundry at Whitechapel. These then remained in place until the total refurbishment to the building in the early 1990s when both clock and bells were thoroughly renovated.

Some authorities have stated that the original clock and bell (either or both) from Old Horse Guards, when discarded, were given as a present to the king's physician, Dr John Turton, who supposedly installed the mementoes in his house at Brasted in Kent.[197] No documentary evidence is known that validates this interesting tradition, nor does Brasted seem to have these antiques today. Interestingly, though, the stable block there has above it the remains of a turret clock engraved 'John Davis, Windsor 1723'. Was this the one Seddon rebuilt? If so, it would only have been about 30 years old at the time of renovation in 1753 and so hardly in the totally irreparable condition described by John Davis himself. Additionally, as noted, the Seddon family claimed to have 'had the care of the Said Clock' for over 60 years, which seems to imply an unbroken continuity of one clock. Hanging above the Brasted clock is a single bell dated '1800', of unknown provenance and clearly not related to the record of timepiece events at Horse

The Horse Guards clock 'of mighty fame directs the dinner of each careful dame'. Many such couplets were penned extolling the perennial accuracy of London's once most exalted timepiece: an accuracy that continues unimpaired today, though popular acclaim may have migrated (in part) to the latecomer, Big Ben. Depicted is the original 1768 movement showing its 'Going' and 'Strike' trains. Horse Guards is possibly the only public clock in London, maybe in the country, having both roman numerals (for the hours), and arabic (for the minutes) on its dial. (Media Operations, HQ London District)

Guards. Very much in the tradition of beds that Queen Elizabeth slept in, there are various other claimants to the tradition of having in their clock towers timepieces that 'were once at Horse Guards', these ranging at present from Purfleet, to Wallingford, to Benson. Unfortunately, as with Brasted, all such claims thus far remain unproven.

Back in London, meanwhile, another link with Whitehall's origins also disappeared at this time when the Holbein Gate sited by the south end of the old Tiltyard was demolished in August 1759. The Duke of Cumberland, as park ranger, had intentions of re-erecting it in Windsor Great Park, but the idea never materialized. The gate had been a bane to traffic using King Street ever since its imposition there in 1530 by Henry VIII. Pepys used to regularly curse the 'great stop of coaches' he encountered there most days.[198]

The first Secretary-at-War to take the War Office permanently into Horse Guards was Viscount Barrington, who held the office from 1755 to 1761 and again 1765 to 1778. Interestingly, Barrington used his new-found authority to prevail upon the

The Bells of Horse Guards. Pictured at the Whitechapel Bell Foundry in London where they were originally cast in 1789/90; the date is 1992, when the chime of bells was taken down for cleaning and re-tuning. Pictured overseeing the operation is Staff Project Officer Lieutenant Colonel R. R. Giles, The Blues and Royals, and Military Knight of Windsor. (Courtesy of The Guards Magazine)

Horse Guards colonel Lord Cadogan, to allow his personal coach to be parked in the new Horse Guards courtyard during his working hours:

> Lord Cadogan's Orders... 16 November 1757... That the Commanding Officers of the Horse Guards at Whitehall Order the Centries always to permit the Secretary at War's Coach to come into the Court Yard at Whitehall, there to remain during the Time His Coach is in Waiting. Also, to let all Gentlemen's Coaches (but no Hackney Coaches) into Whitehall Yard, that have business at the War Office, and when the Coach is Empty, they are to go out of the Court Yard and stand in the Street way. Neither the Secretary at War's Coach, nor any other Gentlemen's Coach, having Business at the War Office be permitted to go thro' the gate into St. James's Park. The Centries are to open the Gates at any time in the Night for the Clerks, whose Business is at the War Office to go in or out.[199]

Probably the most famous event within the new building during its first years was the court martial in February 1760 of Lord George Sackville for disobedience of orders at Minden. His failure to send the cavalry in support of the allied advance led to a verdict of 'Guilty' and a sentence of cashiering further endorsed with the judgement that he was 'Unfit to serve His Majesty in any military capacity whatsoever'.[200]

That same year saw the death of George II; the last British monarch to lead his army in battle. His personal gallantry at Dettingen is always recalled by that name appearing on the Standards and Colours of The Life Guards, The Blues and Royals, the Grenadier, Coldstream, and Scots Guards. These same regiments, on 11 November 1760, performed their ceremonial duty at the King's private internment in Henry VII's chapel at Westminster Abbey.

The accession of George III brought happier times. On 8 September 1761, a Life Guard escort trotted down the Essex to London highway, bringing Princess Charlotte Sophia of Mecklenburg-Strelitz down from Romford for her wedding to the new 22-year old King. A fortnight later the full state panoply of their double coronation brought London to a standstill.

The following year saw Europe stabilized, with the Treaty of Fontainebleau ending the Seven Years' War. The reign of 'Farmer' George was to last 59 years, Queen Charlotte predeceasing her husband by two years. Their life-size portraits continue to dignify the Major-General's office at Horse Guards.

Georgian military matters

ARCH VERSUS COACH

The rapid development of streets in Westminster gradually reduced the role of the Horse Guards arch to usage by royal family members, their accredited courtiers, and the periodic passage of state processions. It must in fairness be added, however, that Household Cavalrymen riding four abreast in Sovereign's escort formation can only just squeeze through it. Then, in October 1762, prior to the state opening of Parliament, a newsletter reported, 'The ground is going to be lowered under the arch at Horse Guards to make room for His Majesty's new state coach to pass through.'[201] The 'new state coach' was in fact the Gold State Coach still in use today. This 'very superb' example of its kind was delivered to the Royal Mews on 24 November 1762 to be readied for the state opening of Parliament the following day. However, while the road lowering had catered for its height (12 feet 10½ inches), the lateral width of the arch was literally 'set in stone'. Thus, when it passed through on the way to Parliament it was definitely a case of 'breathe in!'; with a width of 8 feet 3 inches, it just scraped through, but at the cost of 'one of the Door Glasses and the handle of the Door being broken'.[202]

MAINTAINING LAW AND ORDER

The role of the Household troops at Horse Guards as guardians of civil law and order became progressively more demanding with the growth of the settled population around Whitehall, Westminster and St James's. The sheer number of people that took to the streets on such occasions as the political riots incited by John Wilkes in 1768 taxed London's military resources to the limit. It became a regular practice for a Justice of the Peace to be 'awaiting in the Tiltyard Coffee House' to accompany the Guards should a detachment be sent for.[203] But this was not all bad, for by this time the Tiltyard Coffee House had become one of London's most noted fish restaurants, as Boswell recorded: 'there is no wit except at the Bedford; no military genius but at George's; no wine but at the Star and Garter; no turbot except at the Tiltyard'.[204]

Some civil initiative towards helping the Household Troops was embodied in the 'two pursuit horses with proper pursuers' quartered at Bow Street in 1758. By 1760, Sir John Fielding had organized this unit into a regular mounted patrol, which became the Bow Street Horse Patrol in 1805. These precursors of

The New Horse Guards c.1760. A busy daily scene, with the 2nd Foot Guards (Coldstream Guards) drill and guard-mounting routines in progress in front of their new headquarters. Crossing the Parade are mounted and dismounted Household Cavalrymen from the 2nd Troop of Horse Guards and also the 2nd Troop of Horse Grenadier Guards. The square structure to the left is the sluice gate control for the underground conduit (dug in 1660 by Cromwell's disbanded Ironsides), running under the Whitehall highway which allowed water from high Thames tides to be used to top up the lake in St James's Park. The end of the lake is just visible at top right. At this date it was still a straight rectangular feature in the French style; it was changed to its present curved layout in 1826–27. (J. Chapman, © Queen's Printer and Controller of HMSO, 2005. UK Government Art Collection)

today's Metropolitan Police Mounted Branch gradually appropriated the civil police role assumed by the Guards regiments since the Restoration, leading to a cessation of military street patrols and a reduction of the Horse Guards garrison. In the meantime, though, the Foot Guards of the Tiltyard Guard had been known to punch above their weight (literally) in pursuance of what they considered their public duty. One well-documented instance occurred in June 1770 when a civil bailiff arresting Major-General Gansell of the Coldstream Guards for debt found himself manhandled outside Horse Guards and relieved of his prisoner by Sergeant Bacon and some of his Tiltyard

Guard. Remonstrations by the civil authority went all the way to the top, resulting in the king informing the Field Officer-in-Waiting that he was 'willing to believe they did not know the Major-General was arrested, and only thought they were delivering an officer in distress'.[205] Nevertheless, the Tiltyard Guard commander and the 'rescued' major-general both ended up in jail!

A small prison was located across the highway from Horse Guards in the old Whitehall Palace gateway, the Court Gate. Before its demolition in 1765, it had served as a local lock-up popularly known as 'the Gatehouse'. However, the atmosphere of civil unrest associated with the 'Wilkes & Liberty' street riots fostered by the radical, and troublesome Middlesex MP John Wilkes, led to the construction of a new Gatehouse prison there in 1768. It existed for 45 years before being removed to Upper Thames Street, a consequence of the widening of the Whitehall thoroughfare in 1813. Some authorities have tended to confuse these successive Gatehouse lock-up facilities with the Horse Guards guardhouse opposite: they were separate buildings. The Gordon Riots instigated by Lord George Gordon in June 1780 resulted in the encampment of hundreds of soldiers in St James's Park for several weeks.

In more peaceful times, the Park was still a popular London venue, a German traveller in 1773 describing it as 'swarming in the evening and night with people of all ranks, who promenade up and down the Mall not only by daylight but even after dark by the light of an innumerable quantity of lamps'.[206] Since the death of Queen Anne, however, the Georgian glitterati had taken over the park, and it had reverted to what cavalier rake, the Earl of Rochester, had once described as 'This all-sin-sheltering grove'.[207]

The exercise of law and order in St James's Park was a principal duty of the Foot Guards' Tiltyard Guard that only gradually diminished in the years following 1829, when Sir Robert Peel's new police force set out to cope with a London statistic of one footpad (robber), highwayman, or thief for every 22 inhabitants. By Georgian times, the Park had become a noted gathering place for many such types, as well as for prostitutes, not to mention other distractions such as 'unlawful games, bathings, running of races naked, etc.'[208] One feature of the Park

that contributed further to disorderly situations were the stalls set up for the sale of milk fresh from the cows grazed there, popularly known as the 'St James's Milk Fair'.

Farm livestock had free-ranged across the St James's meadows since medieval times, but the sale of produce from these animals only started when the land became a closed park. Initially only the appointed park rangers were allowed to profit from this perk. By Georgian and Victorian times, however, there existed at least eight milk stands in the summer months and not fewer than four in the winter, all licensed by the Lord Chamberlain. Most were sited along where the Mall now runs. The grazing

The Milk Fair in St James's Park c.1790. Patronizing this long-established public amenity is seen a trooper of the Royal Regiment of Horse Guards. (G. Morland © Yale Center for British Art, Paul Mellon Collection, USA/ The Bridgeman Art Library)

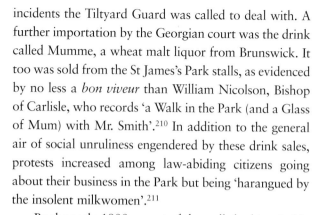

The St James's Milk Fair c.1900. This stall, run by Mrs Orford (seen milking the cow), was the last remnant of a centuries-old tradition and was sited where the Guards Memorial stands today. Petitions to Parliament and letters to the royal household staved off closure for a few years, but the inevitable demise of the amenity took place in November 1922. (Topfoto)

rental applied per animal was about two shillings a week. Stabled in the back streets of Westminster, the cows were herded back and forth each day to the Park through the lesser-populated alleys. The Park scenario of the Milk Fair has been captured on canvas by various artists, though perhaps the best depictions are those of Benjamin West.[209] Although authorized, the supervision of the milkmaids' activities, their appearance and hygiene left much to be desired. Stalls were handed down through family generations, and a very popular (and profitable) sale, at 2d per mug, was a drink called sillabub, which comprised one-third wine, two-thirds milk. Milk on its own cost 1d per mug. With hundreds of people thronging the park each day, it is easy to imagine how sillabub contributed to the many disorderly

incidents the Tiltyard Guard was called to deal with. A further importation by the Georgian court was the drink called Mumme, a wheat malt liquor from Brunswick. It too was sold from the St James's Park stalls, as evidenced by no less a *bon viveur* than William Nicolson, Bishop of Carlisle, who records 'a Walk in the Park (and a Glass of Mum) with Mr. Smith'.[210] In addition to the general air of social unruliness engendered by these drink sales, protests increased among law-abiding citizens going about their business in the Park but being 'harangued by the insolent milkwomen'.[211]

By the early 1900s, most of the stalls had inevitably had their authorization to trade withdrawn, except one run by the redoubtable Mrs Orford.[212] Her family had manned a stall (with cows) in the Park for 250 years. In 1905, however, she was forced to move from the Mall down to a site (with no cows) near where the Guards Memorial now is. Then, when her licence to trade was eventually revoked in September 1921, she raised a large petition to Parliament for retention of her milk stall as a social amenity. Debate in the local press became quite heated, but it was to no avail: the planning for the new Horse Guards approach road was well advanced. On 30 November 1922, the Office of Works took over the site from Mrs Orford, consigning this last link with the origins of St James's Park to history.[213] Today, the Guards Memorial, designed by H. C. Bradshaw, sculpted by Gilbert Ledward and unveiled with great ceremony by HRH the Duke of Connaught on 16 October 1926, occupies the site of Mrs Orford's stall. An interesting pictorial connection between the Household Cavalry and the Milk Fair does exist. The artist George Morland, in his *St James's Park*, depicts a soldier of the Royal Regiment of Horse Guards

patronizing one of the milk stalls in *c*.1790. Whether duty or pleasure took him there is not recorded.

THE COVETED IVORY PASS

With the Court now at St James's, traffic to and from the palace increased significantly. Additional public entrances to the Park were therefore opened, one at Arlington House and another at St James's itself. Further measures were enacted to control vehicular use of the park, including the publication of 'Their Majesties Courts' Carriage Regulations' on the Household Cavalry sentry boxes. The Lord Chamberlain maintained a list of those authorized by the monarch to drive in the Park, and copies were kept at the new gates as well as at Horse Guards Gate.

In 1702, John Sheffield, Duke of Buckingham, purchased Arlington House. He demolished the old structure, replacing it with Buckingham House in 1708. He sited his new house a little further north from the old; also, importantly, he slightly turned his new courtyard frontage so that it was square on to the Mall. This marked the beginning of the Mall's transition from being a Restoration park promenade into the formal royal approach carriageway we know today. There had been a previous additional carriageway across the Park that Lord Arlington (Charles II's Secretary of State) created to ride from Horse Guards Arch to Arlington House. Known as 'The coachway from ye Horse Guard to Arlington House…'[214] it can be seen in Knyff's 1690s view of Whitehall stretching (some 1,400 yards) across the Park. This was remodelled as Birdcage Walk in later Georgian developments.

In April 1762, George III bought Buckingham House for Queen Charlotte, it subsequently being known as 'The Queen's House'. In the 1820s, George IV contracted architect John Nash to convert the house into a palace at a cost that outraged Parliament. Buckingham Palace remained half-finished until Queen Victoria decided to use it as a London residence in 1837. By guarding the entrance to St James's Park, Horse Guards may be said, therefore, to be Buckingham Palace's official entrance; but only insofar as that building forms just one constituent element of Her Majesty's Court of St James's; and it is that entire Court with all integrated buildings which Horse Guards has actually guarded from 1698, and continues to do to the present day. From the Restoration to 1698 of course, as we have seen, it guarded the Court housed in the Whitehall staterooms across the road from where the sentries stand today.

The Tiltyard Guard in St James's Park, 1794. This view, officially entitled The Mall, *shows a Foot Guard sentry from the Tiltyard Guard on peace-keeping duties in the Hanoverian era of the park, itself portrayed at its sylvan best. The sentry box provided for him is one of about a dozen scattered around what is today Green Park and St James's Park: they appear perpetually in the Works accounts requiring repair and renovation. (Jean-Baptiste Chatelain, Guildhall Library, City of London)*

An ivory pass. Engraved in red and for Horse Guards – thus denoting a holder of the most senior status – and issued to allow the bearer, in this case the Prince of Anspach, to ride through Horse Guards arch. To exercise this privilege he would have had to display the pass to the sentries on duty. The pass dates probably from the 1790s at which time Germany was sub-divided into a proliferation of petty principalities. The 'Prince of Anspach' is likely to have been Prince Christian Frederick, Margrave of Brandenburg, Ansbach, and Bareith, Duke of Prussia. He was in London from October 1791 following his marriage to Elizabeth Craven, they lived at Brandenburg House in Hammersmith until his death in 1806. The Margravine Elizabeth became a well-known dramatist of the Hanoverian court and wrote the scripts and music for several plays which she performed in the private theatre attached to Brandenburg House. (Author's collection)

After the new Horse Guards arch entrance opened in 1753, however, policing it became increasingly difficult. The register of names kept in the Guard Houses of the Horse Guard and the Tiltyard Guard was quickly corrupted: entries in the register could be purchased from friends in the right quarters. With the expanding court at St James's requiring the attendance of thousands of persons each year, the decision was taken in 1775 to further refine the procedure for access to the Court through Horse Guards. In a memo dated 14 March 1775, Lord Rochford advised Gold Stick-in-Waiting, Earl de la Warr, of the King's new orders:

My Lord… As there has been a great Abuse in suffering carriages to pass through St. James's Park without the King's permission, I am commanded to signify to your Lordship His Majesty's Pleasure that the Persons mentioned in the inclosed list marked A be permitted to pass in their carriages through the Gates of St. James's and the Green Park; and to avoid as much as possible any Mistake with regard to their Carriages each of those persons has been furnished with Ivory Tickets according to the inclosed pattern on which are engraved <u>Park Gates</u>, with the addition of their respective Names and Titles in Black Characters.

I have the King's command to inclose to your Lordship another list marked B of Persons who are permitted to pass through the Horse Guards and are furnished with Ivory Tickets according to the inclosed Pattern on which are engraved <u>Horse Guards</u> with the addition of their respective Names and Titles in red Characters, and it is His Majesty's Pleasure that the Persons mentioned in the said List marked B be permitted to pass also in their Carriages through all the Gates without exception into and out of St. James's and the Green Park.[215]

Access to the Park by carriage was thus gained only by possession of the approved ivory pass. A degree of selectivity was also retained by adding the name of the gate that could be so used on the pass: by this means only the most privileged could have their ivory passes engraved with 'Horse Guards' in red. This 1775 order has continued to the present day (though ivory has become ivorine), in that persons wishing to pass through Horse Guards arch on wheeled transport will only be allowed to do so on displaying their pass to the sentry. The 'List of Persons enjoying the Privilege of Driving through Horse Guards Gate' is today maintained by the Home Office and remains a prized diplomatic grant. Members of the Royal Family are not listed and do not need passes, St James's Park being perceived as within the Court precincts, and therefore seen as 'their' park.

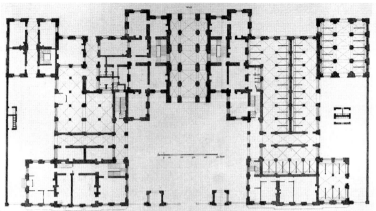
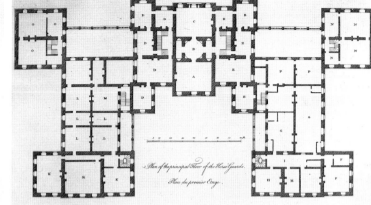

It is to Secretary-at-War Charles Jenkinson (1778–82) that we owe a first glimpse of the inner workings of the Georgian Horse Guards War Office. In July 1782, he had drawn up (at the behest of an inquisitive Treasury) a listing of all personnel in post at that date, defining their responsibilities and remuneration details. Its compilation involved four of the senior clerks who could muster between them 155 years of service to military accounts. Not surprisingly, following such detail proved tortuous in the extreme: do we see here the earliest example of military smokescreen tactics? Certainly, the desired effect was obtained: the Treasury gave up peering into the fog and left the department alone for a long time. Some conclusions can be drawn from the list concerning the seemingly lucrative livings made by these civil servants who controlled large elements of the nation's military forces. One should remember, however, that the system they operated at Horse Guards, while exclusively beneficial to them, was one they inherited,

not created: it had always been done that way, and they had no authority to alter it. At the same time, it was onerous and highly labour intensive and its rewards were well earned. The full transcript is to be found in Appendix B.

Reforms and renovations

An event of considerable significance to the Household Cavalry occurred in 1788, when George III took a long, hard look at his personal bodyguard and was less than satisfied with what he saw. Household Cavalry historian Sir George Arthur summarized the situation:

The corps had long ceased to be composed of noblemen or gentlemen. High birth had been superseded by hard cash as a key for entrance into the Troops of Horse Guards. The change was not for the better and it was felt the time had come for doing away with the pretence to enforce a principle of selection long obsolete.[216]

The occupancy of New Horse Guards, c.1770. As can be seen, both Household Cavalry and Foot Guards are already being squeezed into their respective ends of the building. Also of interest is the confirmation that the Coffee House and the Foot Guards' Sutlers were separate entities. First Floor: A. Chapel; C. Court Martial Room; D. Secretary at War Apartt; E. Judge Advocate Genl; F. Quarter Master's Apartt; G. Horse Guards rooms; H. Horse officers; I. Arms gallery; K. Coffee house; L. Comptroller of Army Accts; N. Paymaster Genls office; O. Commissary General; P. Surveyor's Apart. (Courtesy of the Council, National Army Museum)

To correct these abuses and to restore the integrity of the Household Cavalry, the Troops of Horse Guards were changed into regular cavalry regiments by amalgamating each Horse Guards Troop with its Horse Grenadier troop, the latter having always been regular cavalry. An extract from the Royal Proclamation dated 8 June 1788 defines the change of name of the regiment: 'our First Troop of Horse Guards now under the command of Lt.General the Marquis of Lothian, shall bear the title of our First Regiment of Life Guards, and our Second Troop of Horse Guards, now under the command of General Lord Amherst, the title of our Second Regiment of Life Guards'.[217]

Each regiment, with its initial establishment of 230 men including officers, was to serve in its new name until 1922. The 'Private Gentlemen' who had purchased their entrance into the old Troops of Horse Guards were invited to continue with the new Life Guards regiments; however, many wishing to avoid the implications of regular soldiering declined the offer and were refunded their entrance money. By the end of the 12 months it took to complete the amalgamation, the Treasury had advanced £10,495-11-0 for refunds to the Private Gentlemen of the old First Troop, and £13,335-12-0 to those of the old Second Troop.[218] During the amalgamation year, the guard duties at Horse Guards were performed for the first time by the Royal Regiment of Horse (Blue), or the Royal Horse Guards (The Blues), as they were most often known (today The Blues and Royals). The reformed Life Guards regiments resumed King's Guard from them on 4 June 1789.

Military command in general, and that within Horse Guards in particular, was subject to many and varied reforms during the 50 years following the completion of the new building. The Life Guards' amalgamation was one step in the right direction; Edmund Burke's Act of Economic Reform passed in 1782 was another. Under its provisions, the Secretary-at-War – instead of the commanding officers – assumed control of payment of soldiers and, among other things, recruitment expenditure. Thus it became infinitely more difficult for regimental commanding officers to claim pay for 'men' who existed only as names on a muster roll.

With the onset of the French Wars in 1793, there followed a wave of new military appointments. The post of Commander-in-Chief, which had again reverted to the monarch, was revived in the person of Lord Amherst in 1794. Already ensconced at Horse Guards was the

Secretary-at-War, William Wyndham; now, for the first time, the C-in-C was allocated office space in Horse Guards as well. In 1794, a parliamentary Secretary of State for War (Henry Dundas) was also created with responsibility for general military policy. Authority for command of military matters now veered between the C-in-C as the King's representative, the Secretary-at-War as the government's representative and the new Secretary of State for War – both of the former officials being answerable to the last-named. The Secretary of State for War in fact proved to be little more than a figurehead and became even less involved in the military executive when, in 1801, his post was expanded to that of Secretary of State for War and the Colonies.

This progressive dilution and diversification of military control was reflected in Horse Guards. By 1803, it housed offices for the following officials: the Secretary-at-War, the Commander-in-Chief, the Superintendent of Military Accounts, the Board of General Officers, the Commissary-in-Chief, a returned Judge Advocate General, the Army Medical Board, the newly appointed Barrackmaster General (controlling 42 newly built barracks), the Commissary General of Musters, a Board of Ordnance office, and the Commissioners of Chelsea Hospital, the last-named having being evicted from the Paymaster General's offices.

The Napoleonic crisis of the early 1800s resulted in an army of 151,000 at home and abroad, administered from Horse Guards; consequently, the old problem resurfaced of more officials and fewer rooms for them. The stabling under the Paymaster's office had been relinquished to offices. Even the Sutling House was checked for possible conversion, but the vested interests of the Foot Guards officers ensured

its survival. Perhaps a more influential factor in its continuance was its popularity as an official meeting place for freemasonry lodges. The Royal York Lodge of Perseverance (est. 1776) – associated with the Coldstream Guards from 1793 to 1821 – met at Horse Guards in 1793–94; likewise the Gothic Lodge (est. 1765) met there between 1792 and 1800, and the St Thomas Lodge (est. 1775) met there between 1794 and 1811.[219] That these dates fall almost exactly within the era of the Napoleonic Wars is probably coincidental, but nonetheless interesting.

A Gold Stick Order was issued in March 1801 in an attempt to improve the cramped conditions of the Horse Guards accommodation. The strength of the King's Life Guard was reduced to three officers, one quartermaster, one trumpeter, two corporals of horse, 49 privates, and five light dragoons (see pp.105–106 for the last-named). Some additional office space was eventually found by the relatively simple, but architecturally questionable, expedient of adding two more storeys to the ground floor blocks that connected the wings of the building to its centre. This was done in 1803, only after Secretary-at-War Charles Bathurst had advised the King that he had 'found it necessary to make some alterations for the accommodation of the clerks in my office which may occasion a change in the outward appearance of the building at Horse Guards'.[220]

The design for the altered facade and internal offices was prepared by Thomas Rice, Surveyor of Horse Guards, and approved by James Wyatt, the Surveyor General. Thus the building acquired the outward appearance it has today. One result of the design was that the Secretary-at-War and the Commander-in-Chief occupied office suites on either side of the clock tower.

But they communicated more by memo than by meeting, each at pains to guard his own assumed, rather than defined, sphere of responsibility. This divisive method of double-headed maladministration was to work against the army's best interests at every turn for most of the next 100 years.

In conjunction with the provision of the extra office space, the Household Cavalry guard quarters in the north-east wing were redesigned, as noted in the following order: 'The new guard room at Horse Guards will be used at present as a sitting room by the men on guard, and they will sleep in the rooms upstairs. The room up two stairs, called the powdering room, is to be used as the cleaning room for the guard.'[221] Today, the guard still uses the same rooms 'upstairs' and 'up two stairs' when off duty and for kit cleaning. The 'powdering room' was a relic of the early 18th century, when wigs were powdered and equipment pipeclayed. With regard to wigs, the Tiltyard Guard had, at an earlier date, found itself at the cutting edge of fashion when regimental orders were issued that required the officers 'to appear on Tuesday next, at a review in Hyde Park, and to have on "twisted ramilyed wigs" according to the pattern which may be seen at the Tiltyard tomorrow'. Who in the Tiltyard Guard was ordered to model the desired pattern the records fail to say.[222]

The regimental orderly rooms of the First and Third Guards (today the Grenadier Guards and the Scots Guards) and the Coldstream Guards survived the office space search. They continued to be sited in the south wing of Horse Guards, on the Park side of the building, from whence their staffs administered their respective regiment's duties.

As Horse Guards was being redesigned so the Guards regiments were also undergoing some changes. In London, the duty regiment of Life Guards finding the King's Life Guard at Horse Guards – 51 every alternate day[223] – had its bounds of responsibility redefined as 'both sides of Whitehall and extended on the Parade side as far as the double sentry at Carlton Garden at the end of the Mall'. The double sentry was furnished by the Foot Guards.[224] When the monarch was resident at Buckingham Palace, a four-man piquet of the Life Guard was sent out each evening to round up any malingerers in St James's Park.

Unique to Horse Guards and London is the annual spectacle of the Queen's Birthday Parade – Trooping the Colour – with the centre-piece always being the Colour of the Foot Guards regiment being trooped through their ranks. In present times, when this is concluded, the Mounted Band of the Household Cavalry, led by the two regimental drum horses, takes the centre of Horse Guards Parade to play the walk and trot past music for the King's Troop Royal Horse Artillery and the Household Cavalry. Inevitably, all eyes focus on the gleaming kettle drums atop their towering mounts. The solid silver drums were the gift to the Household Cavalry regiments from this era of the later Hanoverian kings. First to receive theirs was the Royal Horse Guards, from George III on 23 April (St George's Day), 1805. It was a very early parade at 7am at Windsor Castle, preceding the annual installation of the Knights of the Garter ceremony later in the day.[225] George III was so impressed with Royal Horse Guards regiment that he kept them at duty in Windsor for the last 20 years of his reign. The Life Guards regiments received their silver drums in 1831.

OPPOSITE
The Household Cavalry guardroom at Horse Guards in 1831. Depicting a typical off-duty scenario of relaxation for men of the 2nd Life Guards Regiment – today's guard members could easily relate to it! Although given the fair degree of artistic licence, the extensive depiction of equipment and uniform detail is impressive. (F. R. Pickersgill, Courtesy of the Council, National Army Museum)

Life under the clock: A Horse Guards' miscellany

In 1820, a highly significant Household Cavalry event occurred when George IV (r.1820–30) granted The Royal Horse Guards equal status with the first and second regiments of Life Guards. A letter from the Duke of York as C-in-C, to the Duke of Wellington as Colonel of the Royal Regiment of Horse Guards (Blue) defines the King's decision:

> My Lord Duke, I have received the King's Commission to acquaint your Grace that, taking into consideration the distinguished conduct of the Royal Regiment of Horse Guards, Blue, and being fully aware of the partiality which his late Majesty ever entertained for that Corps, his Majesty conceives that he is only fulfilling the intention of his late Majesty in granting to the Regiment the same Honours and Priveleges in every respect as are possessed by the two Regiments of Life Guards, and in consequence of which it is his Majesty's gracious intention that your Grace should roll with, and take your share of your duty as Gold Stick with, the Colonels of those two Regiments; and also that the Field Officers of the Horse Guards should take their share of the duty of Silver Stick.[226]

Consequently, on 14 June of that year the Blues moved up from Windsor to Regents Park Barracks to commence rotational sentry duty at Horse Guards with the two Life Guards regiments.

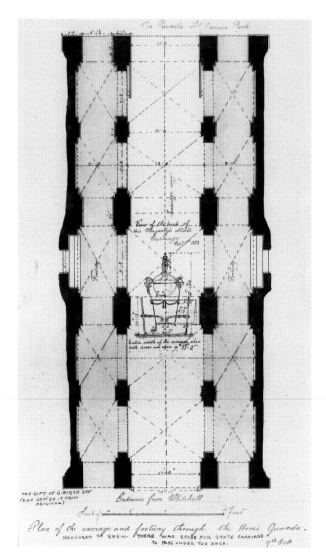

The 'Coach versus Arch' saga – an 1822 episode. The necessary survey preliminary to the passage of the Gold State Coach through Horse Guards arch, in this instance prior to the November 1822 state opening of Parliament. (Courtesy of the Council, National Army Museum, Fairhaven Collection 24709)

At about this date, a French visitor made an assessment of British army administration. He listed the following departments at Horse Guards: a Commander-in-Chief's department, dealing with promotions, commission sales, civil and various affairs (he noted the C-in-C's office expenses increased from £1,029 in 1794 to £9,761 in 1814, obviously due to the 'Napoleon factor'); supporting the C-in-C was an Adjutant-General's department with a Deputy, an Assistant, and a Deputy Assistant Adjutant General, and 11 civilian clerks, three messengers and a housekeeper; a Quartermaster General (QMG), Deputy QMG, and no fewer than five Assistant QMGs, plus seven clerks, one office keeper, and two messengers.[227]

The Public Buildings of London by Britton and Pugin includes a plan of the Horse Guards ground and first floors in 1825. The changed usages by then, in comparison with the original 1760 allocation, make apparent the mushrooming military administrative staff competing for space in Horse Guards. On the ground floor, the Household Cavalry Officers' rooms are now allocated to the C-in-C; also the barber and gunsmith have gone, their rooms being now 'offices'. The Judge Advocate General's rooms were vacated in 1803 when that department removed to Downing Street, and his former suite has become 'offices' and a 'messenger's room'. The latter, incidentally, was described by a visiting contemporary as 'a sombre, ill-lighted den, where at any day or hour may be discovered a messenger, with a corporal of the Foot Guards whose principal duty seems to consist in devouring quantities of bread and cheese washed down by porter'.[228] An interesting perk that War Office

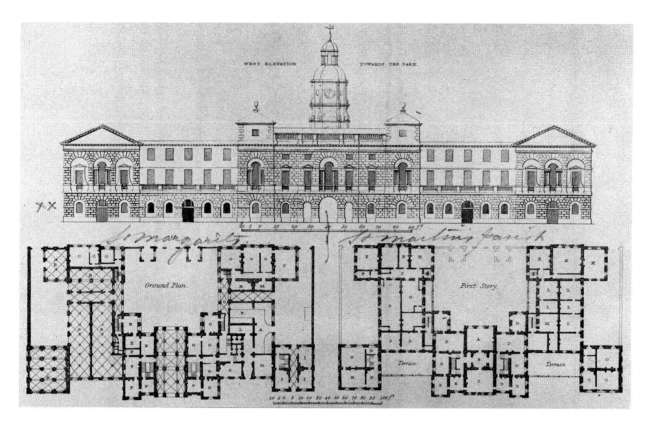

The Georgian military administration – Horse Guards in 1825. Ground Floor: A. Rooms for the Foot Guards; B. Stables for the Horse Guards; C. Sutling Office; D. Arcade; E. C-in-C's Offices; F. Messenger Room; G. War offices; H. Captain's sleeping room; I. Orderly Rooms; K. Rooms for the Foot Guards; L. Orderly room; M. Offices; N. Offices; O. Adjutant General's office; P. Sutling office. First Floor: A. C-in-C's room; B. Vestibule; C. C-in-C's audience room; D. War offices; E. C-in-C's offices; F. C-in-C's offices; G. Horse Guards sleeping room; H. C-in-C's offices; I. C-in-C's offices; K. Coffee/ Sutling House; L. War offices; M. War offices; N. Paymaster's offices; O. War offices; P. Quartermaster General; Q. Quartermaster General. (Courtesy of the Council, National Army Museum, 7405-69-165/166)

messengers enjoyed at this time was their receipt of 5/- cash and 3lbs of candles on days of national celebrations ('occasions of general illumination').[229] On the first floor, the chapel has become the C-in-C's office, while the adjoining room overlooking the parade ground – previously a courts martial venue – is now the C-in-C's audience room. The Foot Guards' three ground floor orderly rooms remain – for Grenadier, Coldstream and Scots Guards.

In 1808, the Guards' place of worship was removed from Horse Guards to the gallery pews of the Chapel Royal in the Banqueting House. It remained here until 1839, when the original Guards chapel at Wellington Barracks was completed.[230] The rooms of the former Comptroller of Army Accounts and the Quartermaster are seen in the 1825 plan as allocated to the 'War Office'. In the north-east wing, the 'Horse Officers' rooms with adjoining 'Arms Gallery' are also given up to the C-in-C's department. From about this date, the carbines used by the guard were stored in a rack under the arcade on the north side of the courtyard and guarded by a sentry. The rack and the sentry – still called 'the Sentry over the Arms' – remain today, but the guns themselves have long been removed. The only departments apparently unaltered are the residual Household Cavalry stables, the guardrooms, and both sutlers and Coffee House. Indeed, the Household Cavalry sutler continues today, modernized of course, and no longer called a 'sutler'. The relevant rooms, however, are more or less where they have always been, and continue in the same role of the past three and half centuries: providing sustenance of commendable variety at the mealtimes of each 24-hour Sovereign's Life Guard. Unfortunately, the Foot Guards' equivalent amenity at Horse Guards has not survived.

As the 1760 plan shows, a public entrance was retained at the south end of the building to perpetuate the medieval pedestrian right of way between Whitehall and St James's. In fact, it allowed continuing access for the public to the Sutling/Coffee House for the benefit of those profiting from it. Some authorities consider the Sutling House and Tiltyard Coffee House as two entirely separate ventures, in fact the latter grew from the former. At all periods of their existence, both jointly and individually, they occupied the same south-east corner of the site, which had always enjoyed this unique civilian access. The ground floor contained the largely military Sutling House, while on the floor above was the largely civilian Tiltyard Coffee House.

With the help of Regency wit and bare-knuckle boxing correspondent Pierce Egan, it is possible to glimpse something of what these patrons experienced at the south end of Horse Guards. In 1824, he paid a visit to 'Child's Suttling House at the Horse Guards, the almost exclusive resort of military men'. (As was customary, the sutler's name, Mr Child, is part of the place name.) Egan describes the scene:

In the entrance on the left is a small apartment bearing the dignified inscription 'The Non-Commissioned Officers' Room'. In front of the bar is a larger space, boxed off, and appropriated to the use of the more humble heroical aspirants, the private men; and passing through the bar, looking into Whitehall, is the *Sanctum Sanctorum* for the reception of the more exalted rank, the golden-laced, three-striped, subordinate commandants, Serjeant-Majors and Serjeants, with the colour-clothed regimental appendants of Paymasters and Adjutants Clerks, *et cetera*. Into this latter apartment we were ushered with becoming respect to their superior appearance, at the moment when a warm debate was carrying on as to the respective merits of the deceased Napoleon and the hero of Waterloo. The advocate of the former seemed unconnected with the army: the adherent to the latter appeared in the gaudy array of a Colour-Serjeant of the Foot Guards and was decorated with a Waterloo medal, conspicuously suspended by a blue ribbon[231] to the upper button of his jacket; and of this honourable badge the possessor seemed not less vain than if he had been adorned with the *insignia* of the most noble order of the Garter.[232]

Spectator to the heated argument that ensued, Egan escaped to the bar, where 'an honest native of the 'Emerald Isle' terminated the war of words, calling for 'half a quartern of gin, with which to qualify a pint of Whitbread's entire'. Together with his new-found Irish friend, Egan then 'seated himself in the room allotted to the private soldiers', where they proceeded to get involved in another exchange with the locals concerning the merits, or not, of the Duke of Cumberland's actions in Scotland in 1745. One participant observed that the Duke's *visit* was, rather, a *visitation*. 'Botheration to nice distinctions', added another Irishman, 'Here Mr. Sutler, be after tipping another half-quartern with which to drink success to the royal visitant.' 'We perfectly understand your allusion', said one from a group of Life-guardsmen; 'perhaps then it may be as well to drop the subject.. This diplomacy was answered by 'a Northern', saying, 'there is already on record against the honour o' your corps a vera serious verdick'. Here the Life-guardsmen 'spontaneously started up', but Egan 'averted the impending storm, ordering the circulation once more of the bottle to offer the toast "Unanimity betwixt the military and the people"'.[233]

This vignette aptly illustrates the unruly intermix of the military and the civilians, the latter able to come and go as they pleased within the Tiltyard sutlers and Coffee House areas. It was a place where much civil disorder originated, but as a military site was inaccessible to the embryo police force. The military only effected control on random occasions, as is evident from the following Gold Stick Order of 1802: 'Disturbances having arisen in the Sutling House of the Foot Guards at the Tiltyard between the men of the Guards, it is ordered that in future no man of the King's Life Guard shall go into the Tiltyard passage leading to the Sutling House on any pretence whatsoever.'[234] The passage mentioned led from the Tiltyard Guard out into the front courtyard of Horse Guards.

As mentioned earlier, Horse Guards Parade was frequently a public arena for disciplinary punishments meted out to defaulting Guards personnel; however, one authority states that George IV himself once made

use of its facilities: 'A man libelled him [George IV] and was found guilty after a court case and sentenced to stand in the pillory set up on Horse Guards parade.'[235] This is the only record found so far that describes the existence of a pillory at Horse Guards. Possibly it may have been set up just for this high-profile case to suitably chasten the failed litigant.

Perhaps the most notable contribution of George IV's reign to his regiments, and indeed to British forces as a whole, was the institution of allocating numbers to soldiers – the one thing no serviceman or woman ever forgets, their number. When the War Office staff at Horse Guards who directed this idea sought to compile a sample soldier's documentation set, they asked the nation's premier military leader, the Duke of Wellington, to propose an identity to write in the sample book. The 'Iron Duke', as he was known, entered the name 'Thomas Atkins', recalling a soldier of his old regiment, the 33rd Foot who, as he lay dying in battle, gasped to his old Commanding Officer, 'It's all in a day's work.' So, on 25 November 1829, each regiment in the army received from Horse Guards its *Register of Services and Description Book of Non-Commissioned Officers and Men*, and following its instructions, each regiment commenced listing its men from number '1' onwards. Revised, the numbering discipline continues throughout the forces today.[236]

Although short, the reign of King William IV (r.1830–37) – 65 years old at his accession – left some significant changes to military life within his Household regiments. In 1831, he decided to change the name of the Scots Guards to Scots Fusilier Guards. A generation later, in 1877, after the regiment and Horse Guards had got used to the change, Queen Victoria altered it back to Scots Guards. The regiment, however, retained some of its fusilier traditions, as indeed it does to the present day. Following his coronation, William appointed himself Colonel-in-Chief of the regiments of Household Cavalry. In recognition of his role, he presented sets of silver kettle drums to the two regiments of The Life Guards. The 2nd Regiment received theirs on 6 May 1831; the 1st Regiment, on 23 July 1831. Both presentations were made in the Windsor Home Park with great ceremony.

Attending to fires hazardous to the Whitehall locality was a regular responsibility of the Horse Guards' duty regiments. In fact, with the London Fire Brigade still in its infancy units of the Brigade of Guards were often the first organized force to arrive and take control of any fire in central London. So it was in October 1834, when the old Houses of Parliament caught fire. Though little of the medieval structure and its irreplaceable masterpieces could be saved, parliamentary leader Sir Robert Peel complimented the Guards from Horse Guards and adjoining barracks who limited the conflagration to the best of their efforts.[237]

During this period some random mentions occur of the Household Cavalry Queen's Guard at Horse Guards coming from their duty to participate in the Queen's Birthday Parade. The last definite such recorded event seems to have been in the 1912 Trooping Ceremony. The Household Cavalry Standard of the Guard would not have been actually 'Trooped' through the ranks in Foot Guards' fashion, but instead, as today, paraded past the saluting dais. On these occasions, at the end of the 'Trooping' ceremony, the Queen's Life Guard returned to its daily duty.

The War Office versus Horse Guards

COURIERS AND CAREERS

During William IV's reign, the search for more and better government office space in and around the Whitehall campus continued. Sir Charles Barry's plans for a new Houses of Parliament, an interior revision of Horse Guards, and for other government buildings formed just a few of many such proposals. Though his new Parliament building went ahead, the administration dithered over a host of competing designs and costs for Horse Guards and other central government departments. Thus it was that in 1840 Secretary-at-War Lord Thomas Macaulay glumly recorded in a diary the visible weekly subsidence of a window in his ancient offices.

Barry's 1847 proposed occupancy plans for the ground-level layout of Horse Guards reveals, just behind the Horse Guards guardroom, a four-stall unit annotated as being 'Light Horse Stables'. This was for the use of the detachment of Line cavalry whose role was to carry confidential despatches between the War Office departments in London, the cavalry HQ garrison at Hounslow, and the royal residences in London, Windsor and Hampton Court. The origins of these Despatch Orderlies, or War Office Letter Party, can be dated to the establishment of the Hounslow garrison barracks in 1793. At this time, Prime Minister William

Pitt created the first barracks (and barrackmasters), with the purpose of removing the military from the social temptations inherent on being billetted on innkeepers. The following year, under the same initiative, the king's stables at Hampton Court were also converted into a cavalry barracks for 200 men and horses. It became the duty of the cavalry regiments stationed at Hounslow to provide men for both Hampton Court guard duty and for the despatch orderlies. This military 'pony express' appears to have been functional right up to World War I, as Lieutenant Colonel R. J. T. Hills says: 'they were produced from the Line regiment at Hounslow down to 1913'.[238] Any members of this Light Horse section being

Horse Guards seen as a war memorial, c.1850. Just one of many schemes proposed with Horse Guards as their focus to commemorate the services of deceased soldiers. (A. Beaumont, The Royal Collection © 2006, Her Majesty Queen Elizabeth II)

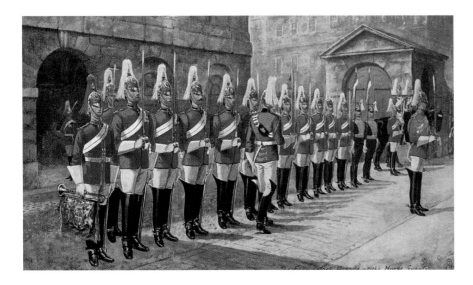

The War Office Letter Party. These postcard views by Harry Payne from the early 1900s show despatch riders from the 21st Lancers firstly, parading with the Queen's Life Guard (formed from the 1st Life Guards Regiment) on the daily 'Four o'clock' inspection parade at Horse Guards, and secondly as a complete piquet of 'Despatch Orderlies' passing Marlborough House on their ride between the offices of the army and the royal court. Interestingly the artist, Harry Payne, served with the 1st Life Guards Regiment in the 1882 Egypt campaign. (Author's collection)

off duty at Horse Guards during the times of Guard Changing, or at the four o'clock inspection in the courtyard, were required to parade in full dress, dismounted, on the left of the Household Cavalry guard. Some contemporary postcards by military artist Harry Payne survive that depict this rare event, showing riders of the 21st Lancers on parade.

From 1842 to 1852, the Duke of Wellington was C-in-C (he had held the post briefly in 1827). In 1849, he caused alarm when he issued a Memorandum from Horse Guards that all existing and future candidates for commissions must be prepared 'to pass an examination before sundry of the Professors at Sandhurst in History and Geography, Algebra and Logarithms, Euclid, French and Latin, Field Fortification, Orthography, and Calligraphy.'[239] It was the beginning of a better, professionally trained and motivated army. Despite this dreaded 'Horse Guards Syllabus', the reputation of the 'Iron Duke' nevertheless continued to be held in the highest esteem. It was a regular feature at Horse Guards during his incumbency as C-in-C that at precisely 4pm, when the groom brought his master's horse under the Horse Guards arch for the ride home to Apsley House at Hyde Park Corner, a large crowd of onlookers would gather to see the old warrior on his way.[240]

The guards at Horse Guards turned out as Queen Victoria and Prince Albert processed across St James's Park on 30 October 1849 to Whitehall and turned down Whitehall Court (today Horse Guards Avenue) to the old riverside Whitehall Stairs: there they embarked by state barge to open the newly built Coal Exchange in the City at Lower Thames Street. This was the last use of the old landing stage which, by then, had probably been in continuous use for upwards of a thousand years, and which represented a last physical royal link with the old Whitehall Palace.

'LAST ORDERS' AT THE TILTYARD SUTLERS

In August 1845, the first concerted attempt was made at officially closing the Tiltyard Sutlers/Coffee House when the Adjutant General proposed the acquisition of the facility to house his office records, which 'have been accumulating for a period of forty six years'. However, he rather diluted his case by adding that 'the building could be carried to greater height with additional rooms introduced into the blank spaces of the building on the north and south sides'.[241] Architect Sir Charles Barry was asked to produce a design, but he failed to adhere to the terms of his commission by proposing instead a monumental front for Horse Guards.[242] Predictably, the Treasury shelved the whole idea – and the Tiltyard Sutlers/Coffee House survived for a few more years.

However, a later communication dated 4 December 1850 between Secretary-at-War Lord Panmure and the Treasury set in motion the process that would finally sound the death knell for the Tiltyard Sutlers/Coffee House. Its opening argument read as follows:

> These rooms since their first erection have been held as the property of the Field Officers of the Brigade of Foot Guards and they are now let at the yearly rent of £312 and the agreement is terminable upon one weeks notice to be given to the tenant by the Field Officers. The Suttling House is not maintained like an ordinary barrack canteen but is to all intents and purposes a common public house and is open till midnight to

The Duke of Wellington, when C-in-C of the army (1827, and 1842–52), giving an audience to a soldier's dependants. The room depicted is the central one over the archway with the Venetian window that overlooks Horse Guards Parade. Subsequently and to the present day the room has served as the office of the Major-General, and Wellington's original desk, as depicted, is still used by the Major-General. On the wall behind and still there today, are pictures of King George III and Queen Charlotte. (Media Operations, HQ London District)

Perhaps unknowingly replicating the Iron Duke's desk-side posture, the current senior military officer in command at Horse Guards, Major-General S. J. L. Roberts, Irish Guards, allows his combat uniform to inform us that a mind for 'sharp end' soldiering needs to be as keen at Horse Guards as in the field. (Media Operations, HQ London District)

persons of all descriptions and is the only instance in which such an Establishment is permitted to exist in a building appropriated to public purposes, the soldiers on guard are forbidden to enter it and generally speaking it is occupied by people of the worst character and low women. The Horse Guards has always been considered as a Military Garrison and formerly the Metropolitan Police were in the habit of visiting the Canteen and reporting upon it but whenever any disturbance took place the Police were constantly brought into collision with the Military who stated that they had no right to enter, it being a Military Garrison and in consequence of this for the last two years the Police have received orders never to interfere and the result has been that the greatest irregularity exists; that people go in and out of the back entrance on Sunday during the hours of divine service and it was only last Sunday that the Sergeant of the Guard was called in to order out some men for making a disturbance and I am informed that for some years past it has been quite a nuisance to the neighbourhood. The question of appropriating this building has been twice mooted first when the Pensions Department was established and then it was relinquished because room was found for them in the Pay Office, on that occasion the Treasury did not object to grant the Field Officers of the Guards that compensation to which the Secretary at War thought they were entitled; and secondly it was thought that the recruiting department might be accommodated there, but there was found not to be room enough...[243]

The proposal concluded with a plan: from the date of the facility's closure, the ten field officers of the Foot Guards who received an income from the Sutling

House would each receive one-tenth of the £312 rent for the remaining duration of their commissions. The loss of rental revenue to the Adjutants of the Life Guards was also compensated. On 24 December 1850, the proposal was approved, thus ending some two centuries of Tiltyard tradition. At the same time, the gates to the south of Horse Guards that had allowed both public and military access to the amenity were taken away and the right-of-way closed for the first time in over five centuries. The rooms released to Horse Guards official usage were occupied by Foot Guards officers and the department of the Clerk of Works. The fate of the 'capital 5-motion beer machine in a neat Spanish mahogany case brass-mounted and with ivory-tipped handles', which formed the centrepiece of this very successful sutler's bar, is unrecorded.[244] As this narrative has shown, the Foot Guards' Sutlers and associated Coffee House had possibly attracted more publicity over the years through its activities than did the military guard it was created to serve.

As shown earlier, Barry's scheme for giving the Horse Guards a more monumental emphasis did not find favour, but others had tried similar ideas. Following the end of the Napoleonic Wars, a number of architects made plans for a national shrine in London to honour the fallen servicemen of the country. In three of the most imaginative schemes, the St James's and Whitehall areas were replanned to incorporate Horse Guards as the focal point of the proposed *place d'armes*. No illustration is known to survive of the earliest, 'A Triumphal Entrance to the Horse Guards designed to commemorate the services of the Deceased', exhibited by W. Wilkins at the Royal Academy in

1837,[245] but plans for the later schemes of Sir Charles Barry (1845)[246] and Alfred Beaumont (1850)[247] still exist and depict clearly the grandiose scale of these projects. Even as recently as 1909, a scheme entitled 'Horse Guards Parade – A Suggested Improvement' was planned by F. W. Speaight and publicized by the Royal Institute of British Architects under the caption 'A British Valhalla'. The national memorial concept underlying all these plans was, of course, destined to find its most potent voice in the 1920 Whitehall Cenotaph of Sir Edwin Lutyens.

As a consequence of the vast military expansion that occurred during the reign of Queen Victoria, Horse Guards was to lose its identity as the traditional sole national authority for military administration. But it continued to be the only choice for great military occasions of state. On 18 November 1852, the Duke of Wellington's impressive funeral cortege started from the Parade (the previous day his coffin had lain in state in the Horse Guards' Audience Room overlooking the Parade). Three years later, Queen Victoria presented medals to the survivors of the Crimean War against a backdrop of Horse Guards bedecked with flags:

She appeared on a dais at the Horse Guards in May 1855 wearing a lilac dress, green mantilla and white bonnet, with Lord Panmure [Secretary of State for War] at her elbow and baskets of medals on blue and yellow ribbons between them. Crowds poured into the Green Park, bands played and a stream of noble fellows, some on crutches some in bath-chairs, rattled past to receive the first Crimean awards. Victoria committed to her journal 'Many of the Privates smiled,

others hardly dared look up ... all touched my hand, the 1st time that a simple Private has touched the hand of his Sovereign... I am proud of it – proud of this tie which links the lowly brave to his Sovereign.'[248]

In fact, the debacle of the Crimean campaign can be taken as the starting point in the radical reorganization of the military administration that ensued and that would engulf Horse Guards.

THE WEST END WAR OFFICE
As a first step, in June 1854, the post of Secretary of State for War was recreated to assume the 'War' role from the Secretary of State for War and the Colonies. The following year, the old post of Secretary-at-War was abolished, its duties being absorbed into that of the new Secretary of State. At Horse Guards, the Commander-in-Chief's departments concerned themselves purely with the military aspects of control (e.g. discipline, orders,

The St James's Park saluting battery. Recorded by the Illustrated London News as celebrating a Crimean victory in 1854 (Alma) and probably taking place near where the Guards Memorial now stands. The ordnance pieces depicted for this salute are defined in artillery language as 'potts', and according to the Royal Artillery, one duty of the staff officer Master Gunner at the Whitehall garrison was 'to fire salutes in the Park.'; the actual 'firing' though, was carried out by an NCO and men of the Coast Brigade, RA, as depicted. When not in use, the 'potts' were kept in 'the Gun House' on the north side of the Parade; one, however, survived to assume a new life (c.1924) as a patio ornament at 7 Whitehall Gardens. (The exemplary placidity of the Household Cavalry officer's charger is astounding!) (Illustrated London News)

The distribution of the Crimea medal by Queen Victoria before a resplendent Horse Guards in May 1855. At this date the medal already had the clasps 'INKERMAN' and 'ALMA'; still to come were 'BALAKLAVA', 'SEVASTOPOL', and the naval clasp, 'AZOFF'. A year later, on 26 June 1856, Queen Victoria awarded the first of her new Victoria Cross decorations, 'For Valour'. Made only by Messrs. Hancocks & Co. from captured Russian gunmetal, at her first investiture the Queen personally decorated 61 recipients: 47 Army, 14 Navy. In respect of the Household regiments, the names on the clasps above (excepting 'BALAKLAVA' and 'AZOFF') appear today as battle honours on the Colours of the Grenadier Guards, Coldstream Guards, and Scots Guards. The Colours of The Blues and Royals display 'BALAKLAVA' and 'SEVASTOPOL'. (Tenniel, Guildhall Library, City of London)

etc). In 1855, these functions of the formerly independent Board of Ordnance were also transferred to the C-in-C. In 1858, the new Secretary of State for War and his civil staff, controlling all matters not supervised by the C-in-C (e.g. legal, provisions, medical, etc), decamped from Horse Guards and took up residence as 'the War Office' at 80–91 Pall Mall. Posted outside was a Foot Guards sentry. The new focal point of the nation's military might – in its cobbled together premises – thus found itself ensconced with such august neighbours as the Carlton Club, founded by the Duke of Wellington, entrance fee £30, and the Reform, £40. This redistribution of responsibility was intended as a corrective, but much had yet to be done to unify a command structure now divided between the C-in-C's Horse Guards HQ and the Pall Mall War Office. The former claimed seniority as the sovereign's military headquarters for most of the past two centuries; the latter proclaimed its authority as the voice of Parliament. The tension between these two bodies often resulted in maladministration. During the Crimean War, Florence Nightingale had been on the receiving end of the resultant chaos. In 1859, she penned her feelings to Secretary of State for War Sidney Herbert: 'The War Department is a very slow office, an enormously expensive office, a not very efficient office, and one in which the Minister's intentions can be entirely negatived by all his sub-departments, and those of each of his sub-departments by every other.'[249]

The situation had to be, and was, radically revised. In 1868–73, the Right Honourable Edward Cardwell was Secretary of State for War, while the C-in-C at Horse Guards was the Duke of Cambridge, first cousin to the queen: both the duke and the queen were opposed to any initiative that would threaten the C-in-C's perceived public status.

Although as Secretary of State for War Cardwell was to initiate his pioneering reforms of the 1870s, his 'enforcer' was his Parliamentary Under-Secretary (P-u-S) Lord Northbrook. The P-u-S was notable for his diplomatic skills and general affability when conversing with his seniors; even the unsuspecting Duke of Cambridge wrote that he thought Northbrook 'a most gentleman-like man with whom it will be pleasant to work'.[250]

Before detailing how the C-in-C was removed from Horse Guards, some observations on the War Office complex in Pall Mall will perhaps add colour to this new locus of British military administration. Collectively, the buildings ran from 80 to 91 Pall Mall: number 80 originally housed the army agency business of Sir John Kirkland, who prospered and diversified to become bankers Holt & Co.[251] At 81 and 82 stood Schomberg House, built in 1698 for King William's

general, the Duke of Schomberg: he was killed on 1 July 1690 in the battle of the Boyne. Subsequently, the house was occupied by artists John Astley, Cosway, painter of miniatures, and no less than Thomas Gainsborough, who lived as Astley's tenant from 1774 until his death in 1788, a period during which he carried out much of his best work. A later (c.1780) occupant of Schomberg was Dr James Graham from Edinburgh, notorious for his self-imposed mission to improve the physical appearance and sexual capacity of his patients. He redefined Schomberg House as the 'Temple of Health and Hymen'. Patronized by the Duchess of Devonshire – who became 'an avid patient' – Graham advertised himself as 'the Servant of the Lord of Wonderful Love'. Employed as a 'goddess' was Emma Hart, who later found fame as Lady Hamilton. The 'Servant' was soon to return to Edinburgh under lunacy surveillance. Next to Schomberg House were nos. 83 and 84 where James Christie, founder of the eponymous auctioneers, lived

The last return from duty. Precisely at 4pm, after each working day at Horse Guards, the 'Iron Duke' would mount his charger and ride home to Apsley House at Hyde Park Corner. Here, in 1852, he is depicted making the journey for the last time with his old groom, John Mears, in attendance. Just visible through the arch is the Queen's Life Guard turned out for the occasion. (Topfoto/ Woodmansterne)

in 1766; by the 1850s, the Board of Ordnance had acquired these houses. From 1760, Cumberland House covered the sites of 85 to 87, being built for the Duke of York, brother of George III; it too was acquired by the Ordnance in 1806. Some shops occupied nos. 88 to 90, abutting which was no. 91, Buckingham House. Built by Soane in 1780 for the Marquess of Buckingham, it became the home of the Duchess of Gordon. In June 1780, her son, Lord George, initiated some of the worst riots ever seen in London, involving hundreds of Household troops in their suppression – Charles Dickens' *Barnaby Rudge* supplies full details.[252] Finally, among this milieu of ghosts was Mistress Eleanor Gwynne. On retirement from the stage, Nell was fitted up by her monarch with a comfortable town house abutting the west wall of Buckingham House, wherein she lived with Charles's illegitimate sons, the Beauclerk boys. The staid diarist John Evelyn thought her 'an impudent comedian' when she called to the king over her garden wall as he walked in St James's Park.[253]

'HORSE GUARDS, PALL MALL'

In 1869, Lord Northbrook went straight to work with his inquiry into the 'Conduct of Business in Army Departments'. This resulted in three executive reports in March and May 1869, and in February 1870, on the basis of which was drafted Cardwell's War Office Act of 1870. This act had as its main plank that the responsibility for all aspects of army administration must reside ultimately in the Secretary of State for War. The most contentious issue was making the Commander-in-Chief subordinate to political – as opposed to regal – control, a change that would be symbolized in moving his office from Horse Guards to Pall Mall. The War Office Act came into force on 4 June 1870;[254] by August 1871, the move of the C-in-C had been accomplished. Extracts from a series of letters between the Duke of Cambridge and the various participants to the move, both for and against, illustrate clearly how Cardwell's War Office Act was viewed and progressed. Sir Robert Biddulph, Master of the Household, communicated the Queen's wishes:

> 2 March 1869... To Mr. Cardwell... Anything that could tend to lower his position in the eyes of the public would, the Queen feels, be a misfortune... She means the removal of the Military Departments of the Army from the Horse Guards to Pall Mall: such a step could not fail to damage the position of the Commander-in-Chief, tho' it might be desirable to build a new office for the Secretary of State [for War] on the site of Dover House, and in connection with the Horse Guards.[255]

As Commander-in-Chief 1856–95, the 39 years in post of the Duke of Cambridge is by far the longest of any incumbent. An old soldier with ingrained standards, he fought the good fight to maintain Horse Guards as the centre of military operations, but the tides of change through which he struggled gamely to swim eventually overcame his resolve. His later biographer listed some 50 radical proposals the Duke had promoted, many of them years ahead of their time – a medical corps, reserve forces, education, magazine rifles. From his statue, designed by Adrian Jones, he maintains an avuncular affinity with his old headquarters nearby. (Topfoto)

On 5 December 1869, the Duke of Cambridge made his feelings about the forthcoming proposal clear to Cardwell:

I feel it a duty I owe to myself as the military representative of the Crown to bring to your notice, in the most forcible manner in my power, the grave objections I entertain against the removal of the Commander-in-Chief from the Horse Guards to the War Office in Pall Mall, and also the substitution of Board meetings for the ordinary War Office meetings.[256]

And further, on 27 December 1869,

If the Secretary of State had a room at the Horse Guards, as the Secretary at War used to have, whilst the Commander-in-Chief had another in Pall Mall, there would be more give-and-take in the arrangement.[257]

With the duke endeavouring to postpone the imposition of this 'Magna Cardwell', a stand-off ensued until the War Office Act came into force the following June. He again called on reinforcements in the form of his cousin the Queen to support him; on 29 January 1871, he received instead the following ambivalent response from the Master of the Household, Sir Thomas Biddulph:

The Queen expresses herself willing to allow a temporary arrangement to be made with reference to the transference of the offices to the War Office, provided it is temporary, and that Y.R.H.'s accommodation is separate, with a separate entrance, and is still called the Horse Guards.[258]

Lord Cardwell. His army reforms of the 1870s emptied Horse Guards of the Commander-in-Chief's department, to the consternation of Queen Victoria whose cousin, the Duke of Cambridge, was C-in-C from 1856 to 1895. However, Cardwell's revolutionary revision of the army structure in assigning regimental units to county bases remained virtually unchanged for the subsequent 100 years. (Topfoto/HIP/British Library)

Cardwell discerned a chink in the opposing royal armour. While Cambridge was on leave abroad, his deputy, Sir Richard Airey, continued to field questions on the move but kept the Duke informed:

21 August 1871 ... to Y.R.H... Mr. Cardwell asked me to call today ... with regard to the maintenance of the appellation of 'Horse Guards', he said he hoped Y.R.H. would not press it; but, if you did, he would sanction our letters being dated 'Horse Guards, War Office'.[259]

But it was all to be of no avail, as this message clearly shows:

General Forster to Sir Edward Lugard, Horse Guards 29 August 1871... I have looked over the apartments

The Gun House on Horse Guards Parade. Sited just to the north of Horse Guards in Spring Gardens and facing on to the Parade, the Gun, or Gunner, House existed from c.1667 to its final demolition in 1885 to make way for the Admiralty enlargement. It originally housed the residence of the Master Gunner of Whitehall and St James's Park, together with a detachment of coastal artillerymen whose role was to service (and fire if necessary) the ordnance pieces sited to defend the Palace of Whitehall. By the 1720s, this role had become redundant and just saluting 'potts' were retained and fired across the park for ceremonial purposes. Following the Cardwell reforms of the 1870s, the Gun House offices housed the newly formed staff of the Major-General commanding the Home District. This latter administrative body moved into the vacated C-in-C's offices at Horse Guards in 1871 and later assumed its present title of Headquarters London District. (J. Crowther, Guildhall Library, City of London)

at the War Office intended to be occupied by the establishment of the Commander-in-Chief, and with every possible desire to facilitate the move of the Officers and Clerks to the War Office, I trust I may be permitted to remark, in H.R.H.'s absence, that until the bridge of communication in course of construction is completed the transaction of business will be very much delayed and will be attended by very serious inconvenience. H.R.H. will be in England on the 5th prox.; and I would request a delay of a very few days before the change takes place.[260]

So, despite entrenched opposition from the Court, the Secretary of State's guile proved equal to the duke's intransigence. Cardwell's War Office Act of 1870 saw the C-in-C made subordinate to the Secretary of State, and his office moved from Horse Guards to Pall Mall, the object being to create a closer physical liaison (via

'the bridge'?) between the two departments. But removal of the C-in-C from Horse Guards did not remove the C-in-C from the debate. When Cardwell left office in 1874, he still left an army with its command divided between two different authorities – the Duke of Cambridge (still as C-in-C) and the Secretary of State for War. It was to stay that way for another 20 years until the duke's retirement in 1895: then, and only then, could the office of Commander-in-Chief be consigned to history. (Whilst at Pall Mall, the Duke headed his letters 'Horse Guards, Pall Mall'.)

Hot on the heels of his War Office Act, Cardwell produced his Army Regulation Bill, which was mainly concerned with the abolition of the promotion purchase system; during the final year of his tenure, he also created his Localization System, or 'Cardwell System', as it became known, which founded the countrywide regional regiments and reserve forces. His plan divided the country into 80 military districts – 66 infantry, 12 artillery and two cavalry – every district having its own regimental depot: many still survive. The staff at Cardwell's administrative offices based at Horse Guards played a vital role in the implementation of all these revolutionary national measures.[261]

The first real test of the new War Office, which at this time comprised some 80 or so officers and about 700 civil servants, came in 1882 with the Egyptian Revolt. Although an effective force was quickly raised and sent to subdue the uprising, various deficiencies of communication in the departments of higher command were still apparent. A commission examining the situation in 1889 under Lord Hartington recommended the creation of an Army Council to replace the two-headed system at Pall Mall. This proposal was seconded by Lord Elgin's commission of 1901 enquiring into similar defects encountered during the South African War; a conflict about which Kipling tersely rhymed, 'We have had no end of a lesson: it will do us no end of good.'[262] Finally, in 1904 the first Army Council was created under the chairmanship of the Secretary of State for War. The post of Commander-in-Chief, first created in 1660, was finally abolished. There had been 21 incumbents of the post; following the Duke of Cambridge, the post had been held by Lord Wolseley, 1895–1900, and Lord Roberts, 1900–04.

Meanwhile, at Horse Guards the representation of the Household Troops also continued to diminish. Enough space had been won to retain the most senior administrative offices for the Guards regiments, and indeed they continue there today; however, one casualty was the Foot Guards' Tiltyard Guard: it mounted for the last time on 15 November 1898, so ending a duty

The Guards Memorial faces Horse Guards across the Parade Ground. Its guardian bronze representatives of the five Foot Guards regiments keep an unwavering eye on today's occupants of their old headquarters. Reciprocally, those occupants heed the message of the monument's ever-reminding presence, silhouetted against the trees of St James's Park. Its 36-foot high, 170-ton form was dedicated there by HRH the Duke of Connaught on 16 October 1926. Designed by H. C. Bradshaw, its bronzes were sculpted from the metal of captured German guns by Gilbert Ledward. By the Duke on the day stood centenarian Grenadier, General Sir George Higginson, thirty years with his regiment, Crimean veteran, and Home District commander 1879–84. (© Michael John Kielty/Corbis)

that had commenced at the Restoration. Interestingly though, the southern Foot Guards' wing of Horse Guards continued to be identified as the 'Tyltyard' in Works accounts up to World War I.[263] In 1881, the Foot Guards' regimental orderly rooms at Horse Guards – having continuously occupied the same small suite of

The then new War Office under construction c.1899. Designed in 1898 by William Young and seen to the right of the photo emerging from its foundations, this 'state of the art' building was completed after his death by his son in 1907. Intended to replace the Pall Mall headquarters and its various offices scattered around London administering the army, it was already out of date by the outbreak of war in 1914. (Author's collection)

rooms in the south wing since the Restoration – moved into renovated rooms previously occupied by the Sutler on the ground floor of the Whitehall side. They remained here for only 20 years; then in December 1901, these three regimental orderly rooms (for the Grenadier, Coldstream and Scots Guards) finally moved out of Horse Guards to improved premises at Buckingham Gate.[264]

For the Household Cavalry, accommodation existed only for a 'full guard' (provided when the monarch is in London residence, when not, a 'short guard' mounts) plus the War Office Letter Party mentioned earlier; overall, this left perhaps a couple of spare horse stalls. The 'full guard' at this time comprised a captain, a subaltern, a corporal major, two corporals of horse, one corporal, one farrier, one trumpeter and 27 troopers.

All other rooms in the building were given over to the use of various War Office and Works staff: these held posts at the cutting edge of the technology of the day and were disguised behind acronyms equal in obscurity to any adopted by their present-day successors. For instance, DWF (CS) translates as 'Director of Works (Fortifications) Civil Staff', who is assisted by an ADWF (CS). IGF concealed the 'Inspector General of Fortifications', while from DWB emerged the 'Director of Works (Buildings)'. IIS was the 'Inspector of Iron Structures' who worked closely with the ISM, 'Inspector of Subterranean Mines'. Many supporting staff appear in the contemporary building plans as draughtsmen or surveyors, or in various roles in the Railway Branch, the Iron Branch Apparatus department, the Defences of London Room, DWF Model Room and the Telegraph Office. Most of these senior posts at Horse Guards were filled by officers of field rank or above, while their opposite numbers in the civil service at Horse Guards were drawn from the senior grades of their profession.

Interestingly, during these early 1900s, while most other offices were being moved from Pall Mall to the new Whitehall War Office building, records exist showing that a Guards' administrative HQ had previously hived itself off from the adjoining Pall Mall complex. Mentioned is 'The Brigade Office, 23 Carlton House Terrace', or the 'Horse Guards Annexe, Carlton House Terrace'. This 'Carlton'-based Guards' HQ formed the original limit of the Horse Guards' guard patrol beat (as described on p.98). It certainly continued there after World War I, according to Guards orders from 1919, but its final closure date remains, at present, unclear.

A tradition for modern times

An early initiative of King Edward VII (r.1901–10) was to address the duties carried out by the Household Troops, principally their responsibilities at Court and at Horse Guards. Through years of inertia, many procedures inherited from the previous reign had become embedded, almost as permanent implants, in the regimental order books. As the vibrant 'Edwardian' court lifestyle began to permeate the renovated state rooms and galleries of St James's and Buckingham Palace, so the dust and detritus, both literal and administrative, of previous years was cleared away.

At Horse Guards, the Household Cavalry had provided a full guard continuously each year, from 9 November to the following September. In September, it was reduced to a short guard, handing over the Horse Guards building for about a month's cleaning and running repairs, until 9 November came round again. The guard during this 'house keeping' month comprised two NCOs and 12 men: probably the genesis of the 'short guard'. During Edward VII's reign, the procedure was substituted for a 'full' or 'long' guard (as earlier described) only to be mounted when the King was in residence in London. When he left town, it reduced to a 'short guard'. The same still happens today. Within the senior officers the newly

Horse Guards sentries c.1909. Note the carbine carried by the mounted sentry: these were discontinued in Edward VII's reign in favour of the cavalry sabres seen today. The carbines were originally stored in a rack behind the foot sentry patrolling under the north arcade of the courtyard and gave him the identity 'The Sentry over the Arms'. Today only the rack for the arms remains in situ, but the sentry still retains his original title. The proclamation notices pasted to the sentry boxes continue the link with the practice of pasting orders for the military on Old Horse Guards gate, and the prior posting of public notices on the original Whitehall Tudor Court Gate opposite. The regiment finding the King's Life Guard is the Royal Horse Guards (the Blues). (Author's collection)

New shoes for Queen's Guard. The Farrier Quartermaster Corporal of the 2nd Life Guards Regiment calms a restive horse being re-shod for Horse Guards duty in 1900. These Victorian farriers would be completely at home in the regimental forge today – so little has changed in the practical terms of their craft. The equine medical care, however, is now a world away from then. Nor would they find any change in the regimental dictum, then as now, 'Horses first'. (Author's collection)

created posts of Silver Stick Medical Officer and Silver Stick Quartermaster respectively had care of 'the sanitary condition of all quarters, guard rooms, etc. in the joint occupation of the Household Cavalry'. The Silver Stick-in-Waiting is deputy to either of the colonels of the Household Cavalry regiments – the Gold Sticks-in-Waiting.[265] The Silver Stick-in-Waiting is also a regular army officer serving at Horse Guards as Commander Household Cavalry. The two subordinate Silver Stick posts of Medical Officer and Quartermaster did not reappear post-1918.

As the army grew so, in proportion, did the War Department staff needed to look after it. Indeed clerical administration of the army had advanced in giant strides since the day in May 1647 when Colonel Sexby had recommended the Council of the Army to recruit 'a partie of able penn men ... imployed to satisfie

and undeceive the people'.[266] While Horse Guards by now housed some 86 executive officers, all with subordinate staffs, by the turn of the 20th century the Pall Mall headquarters had also long since outgrown its capacity. One authority described the conditions there as 'a tiresome jumble of rambling passages, sudden stairs and confusing turns'.[267] Additionally, since 1710 the army's civil staff had occupied yet another 'War Office' building at 7 Whitehall Gardens, into which by now were crammed some 53 officials.[268] To accommodate this ever-growing empire of the Secretary of State for War, the Whitehall War Office building sited opposite Horse Guards – today 'the Old War Office' – was built between 1899 and 1906 (on the site of the old No. 7) to provide about a thousand rooms ranged along $2^1/_2$ miles of corridors. In 13 of these rooms could be found 18th-century marble chimney pieces removed from the Pall Mall offices.[269]

During all these War Office constructions and changes, preparations for the coronation of Edward VII were under way. William Cavendish Bentinck, 6th Duke of Portland, wrote to Crown Equerry Colonel Ewart expressing his concern that the coronation state coach would not fit under the Horse Guards arch on Coronation Day, 9 August 1902: he said he had experienced a dream to that effect. Measurement of the arch confirmed the duke's premonition; the resurfacing of the road over the years had raised the surface by nearly two feet. Perhaps recalling 1762, hasty adjustments were made immediately, and on the day, all went well.[270]

Anyone attending guard mountings at Horse Guards after the South African War in 1901 cannot have failed to notice that one of the horses wore a

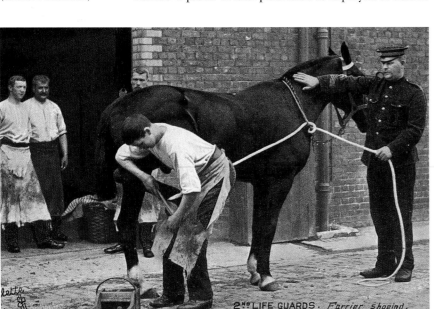

2ND LIFE GUARDS. Farrier Shoeing.

campaign medal on its harness: this horse was 'Freddy'. On 29 November 1900, the troopship *Hawarden Castle* brought home the Household Cavalry regiment from the Boer campaign. Also on board was 'Freddy', the only horse to go to South Africa and return fit for state duty after a due period of rest and convalescence. A 2nd Life Guards horse with regimental number D36, 'Freddy of Paardeburg', as he became known, was officially awarded the Queen Victoria South Africa Medal 1899–1902, with clasps for each of the five campaigns he was in. His medal, together with a full account of his active service, can be seen today in the Household Cavalry Museum. All Household Cavalry horses have two numbers: their four-digit army number is imprinted on their hind hooves, and their regiment and regimental number on their fore hooves. On enlistment, each

horse is also given an official name. Since 1950, all horses enlisted during the same financial year have names starting with the same letter. Reputedly the oldest Household Cavalry horse known to have served on ceremonial duty was Black Velvet of the Royal Horse Guards, being aged 29 when eventually retired in 1966.

Anyone looking out of Horse Guards' courtyard towards Whitehall in June 1907 would have seen the erection of the memorial statue to the old C-in-C, the Duke of Cambridge. The statue was sculpted by Captain Adrian Jones, former Veterinary Surgeon to the 2nd Life Guards Regiment. It is a nice irony that the decision was made to site it midway in the Whitehall thoroughfare, on a point exactly halfway between the Horse Guards and the then new War Office building; thus seeming to perpetuate the controversy of the duke's political position in the Cardwell years of Horse Guards versus War Office.

THE HORSE GUARDS IN WAR AND PEACE

By the outbreak of World War I, the Horse Guards building was just one part of the national military effort co-ordinated from the War Office, though clearly events concerning Guards regiments were viewed with a special interest by Horse Guards' occupants. One such event occurred on 26 October 1914, with the last ever mounted action of a complete Household Cavalry regiment. On this day, the Blues

'Freddy of Paardeburg' c.1902. Seen after his return from the South African War preparing for state duty, and wearing on his harness his officially issued campaign medal with clasps. His medals, and the story of this 2nd Life Guards Regiment horse, can be seen in the Household Cavalry Museum. (Author's collection)

rode to the rescue of the 20th Infantry Brigade at Kruiseecke, near Ypres, across the front of two German cavalry regiments, the latter were too startled at the audacity of the manoeuvre to interfere. The brigade was saved, at a cost to the Blues of eight men and 25 horses.[271] The war years also saw the Household Cavalry 'King's Guard' at Horse Guards reduced to a short guard for the duration, following an order from King George V. This reduced guard comprised one corporal of horse, one corporal, and 13 troopers. In continuing its role of sentry duty at Horse Guards during the Great War, the Household Cavalry guard should not be viewed as purely traditional and decorative. Horse Guards was a highly important headquarters building and a high security risk: many very senior officials worked in its rooms. Additionally, contemporary comments about the Horse Guards sentries evading service abroad by choice were unequivocally rebutted at the time. A statement issued to the press revealed that the King's Life Guard was formed from men who had been invalided from the front, or who were re-enlisted men unable to serve abroad under the conscription terms. Emphasizing this point, the War Office gave special permission for a first issue of the '1914 Star' to those of the Household Cavalry home regiment (nearly all) who were entitled to it. This first official issue in the army of the so-called 'Mons Star' to home units of the Household Cavalry took place on Horse Guards Parade early in 1918. Sixty years earlier, Queen Victoria had issued the Crimea medal to her soldiers on the same spot.[272]

Following the Armistice, some return to London military normality was displayed when, on 3 June 1919, the ceremony of Trooping the Colour resumed its performance. Due to extensive renovation works associated with the Horse Guards approach road, it was not held on Horse Guards Parade; instead the spectacle was performed in Hyde Park. The Trooping returned to Horse Guards permanently in 1921.

A further procedural revision instituted at this time was the change in the system for allocating numbers to soldiers. In the old system, numbers were allocated by regiment; now the numbers would be allocated by the War Office. The former method had resulted in soldiers acquiring several numbers as they moved between regiments. Now, all soldiers were given a unique six-digit number from the central War Office list; this was again revised to an eight-digit number in July 1947 – and which continues today. The Horse Guards' staff was kept fully occupied dealing with the renumbering task across the seven Guards regiments.

With the cessation of hostilities, the financial cost began to be counted; clearly many regiments faced disbandment. In 1922, the two separate 1st and 2nd Life Guards Regiments had to bow to the inevitable and were amalgamated to form one regiment named 'The Life Guards (1st and 2nd)'; in 1928, the name changed to its present form, The Life Guards. The practicality of amalgamating the two 1788 regiments was clear to modern eyes: just one reason was that 14 regimental differences existed between their uniforms and equipment. Also, they occupied two barracks: Regents Park and Hyde Park Barracks, this too was rationalized when in 1932 the former was vacated in favour of the latter.

Sadly, the spectre of European conflict was to rise again, and on 1 September 1939, just before the declaration of hostilities, the King's Life Guard at

Horse Guards, found by The Life Guards, mounted on foot and in service dress khaki for the first time: review order was not to be worn again by the Guard until 1947. Horse Guards received significant bomb damage during World War II – principally on 20–21 February 1944 when hit by three bombs. The King's Life Guard was suspended until suitable repairs were effected; many of the splinter pockmarks still dignify Kent's solid façade, forming, in effect, the

A war-time 'khaki' guard at Horse Guards. The first such guard had been mounted on general mobilization on 1 September 1939. The present-day uniform – known as Mounted Review Order – was not worn again until 1948. (The Household Cavalry Journal)

The American contribution to Horse Guards. The US citizens and their vehicles officially comprising the *1st American Motorized Squadron* (unofficially the 'Red Eagles'), came of age as a recognized Whitehall Home Guard force at this inspection at Horse Guards by Prime Minister Winston Churchill in January 1941. Also depicted is their commanding officer Brigadier General Wade Hampton Hayes. A Virginian, he fought in the 1898 Spanish American War and was staff officer to General Pershing in World War I. (The Times)

building's own personal battle honour. A major casualty of the damage was the Household Brigade Office archives, which were lost in the flooded cellars. During the war years when the King's Life Guard did mount at Horse Guards, its members were conveyed back and forth, to and from Hyde Park Barracks, in furniture vans and old buses. In the period when the King's Life Guard was temporarily suspended, the Corps of Military Police provided the necessary security protection for the Horse Guards building.

In July 1940, after the Fall of France, some of the 4,000 Americans living and working in London decided to form their own unofficial Home Guard unit. Organized by Charles Sweeney – a private to colonel World War I veteran – some 70 men armed themselves with imported guns from the USA and patrolled the London streets in their own American cars 'of high power', painted in camouflage. After this initial 'tommy

gun' incarnation, and following training by Guards instructors, the unit received formal recognition in the September by the GOC Sir Bertram Sergison-Brooke. Now uniformed (and armed) in conformity with the British Home Guard, but with a red American Eagle sleeve badge, the unit – called the 'Red Eagles' – started guard duty in central London. At Horse Guards, it provided the Home Guard protection for one day in six. Its other assumed role was to assist in the personal protection of the London District Commander-in-Chief in the event of an invasion alarm. The Red Eagles continued in operation until 1 November 1944 when they, and the English Home Guard, were stood down. Garments personalized with American Eagles and Scots Thistles are among the unique momentos which belong to the Guards officers who trained the Americans.[273]

At the end of the war, with most of the regimental manpower still on the Continent and undergoing the demobilization process, the guard was formed from a composite regiment at Knightsbridge; both Life Guards and Blues took duty at the same time at Horse Guards. By the summer of 1947, however, the mounted regiment had grown again to its two separate squadrons, and the daily alternation of the two regiments on Horse Guards duty was recommenced.[274] In that same summer, on Thursday 12 June, the first post-war 'Trooping the Colour' ceremony was held. The Foot Guards regiments on parade were dressed entirely in battledress, while the Household Cavalry was in its equivalent service dress. The first post-war occasion when the Household Cavalry was given limited permission to once again wear full ceremonial dress occurred on 7–9 August 1947, for the Liverpool Tattoo; King George VI subsequently approved a permanent return to full dress uniform for the wedding of Princess Elizabeth to Prince Philip on 20 November 1947, and from then on for the Sovereign's Life Guard.

Another significant ceremonial event occurred opposite Horse Guards on 30 January 1949, which kept faith with the unique national historical associations of this particular point in Whitehall. On this date – the tercentenary of the execution of King Charles I – the members of the Royal Stuart Society assembled in front of the window of the Banqueting House nearest the scaffold's site and said prayers in remembrance. The Governor General of the Society then placed a wreath against the outer wall, and a trumpeter of the Royal Horse Guards stood in front of the window and sounded the Last Post and Reveille.[275] The Royal Stuart Society continues annually its remembrance service at the statue of Charles I at the top of Whitehall.

A further consolidation of regimental presence at Horse Guards occurred in 1953, when the Silver Stick-in-Waiting was, for the first time, granted his own administrative department – RHQ Household Cavalry – within the building. The RHQ move to Horse Guards was followed in the same year by that of the Household Cavalry Records Office, which was installed in the rooms above those of the guard in the north wing. Central command of the regiments of the Household Cavalry had returned to its Restoration place of origin. Previously, from 1947, this control had operated from Hyde Park Barracks in Knightsbridge; now, all the affairs of the Household Cavalry regiments, both ceremonial and armoured, were once again managed from Horse Guards.[276] Just 30 or so years later, in 1985,

further Ministry of Defence mandates were to require that many of the functions of the Horse Guards Records Office be relocated to a centralized MoD unit elsewhere in the country.

The Household Cavalry regiments were to undergo another peacetime transformation when, in response to Treasury cost dictates, further amalgamation measures were imposed. On 29 March 1969, at Detmold in Germany, the announcement was made that the Royal Horse Guards regiment was to join with the Royal Dragoons to form a new regiment, The 'Blues and Royals'. On the uniforms of The Blues and Royals sentries at Horse Guards today can be seen the insignia of an eagle standard worn on the upper arm. This denotes the French Eagle belonging to the 105th Ligne

21st-century Horse Guards. As it has been for the last five centuries, Horse Guards' site continues today as the most fitting and evocative backdrop of choice for pageantry and spectacle, both in celebration and mourning, performed in the capital on behalf of the nation. Here, in April 2002, the funeral cortege of Queen Elizabeth the Queen Mother passes through Horse Guards. (Topfoto/PA)

Keeping the peace at Horse Guards, c.1970. Exemplary evidence that the Horse Guards' sentries have always had, as part of their duty role, the containment of incidents within the Horse Guards precincts they consider likely to lead to civil disorder. Here, the dismounted sentry intervenes in a pavement fight between a bus conductor and one of his passengers. The nearby mounted sentry's horse became agitated by the struggle, resulting in the depicted sentry reportedly saying to the conductor, 'Cut it out, or I'll join in!' (Mirrorpix)

captured at Waterloo by Captain Alexander Clark and Corporal Stiles, both of the Royal Dragoons, a trophy that resides in the National Army Museum, Chelsea.[277] The Household Cavalry was further revised by a 'Union' between the armoured regiments of The Life Guards and The Blues and Royals on 19 October 1992: the soldiers remain separately badged but serve together as one united regiment. Later, in another 'joining together', on 18 December 1998, a formal 'twinning' agreement was signed between the Household Cavalry Mounted Regiment and their French opposite numbers Le Régiment de Cavalerie of the Garde Républicaine. Thus the old Napoleonic antagonists finally sealed their reconciliation.

In 2 April 1969, another Household Cavalry precedent occurred when the monarch, for the first time, carried out the inspection of the Queen's Life Guard. Although in a duty role they had not been represented at Horse Guards by a standing guard since 1898, the Foot Guards regiments continued to be administered from there. After the world wars and other actions in which they served with unswerving valour, their regiments, too, were subject to sweeping manpower cuts as every post-war decade passed, even to the time of writing.

THE CHANGING OF THE QUEEN'S LIFE GUARD

From an original total of 108 Household Cavalrymen being on duty from Horse Guards in Restoration times, today only sufficient space remains for a Sovereign's Life Guard of 16 all ranks (a 'long guard') to be mounted there each day. The Queen's Life Guard duty is alternated daily between the two Household Cavalry regiments of The Life Guards and The Blues and Royals. The Life Guards wear scarlet tunics and white plumes; The Blues and Royals, blue tunics and red plumes. Each keeps guard at Horse Guards for 24 hours. When the sovereign is in residence at Buckingham Palace, the Queen's Life Guard comprises one officer, one corporal major, who carries a squadron Standard, one corporal of horse, one corporal, 11 troopers and a trumpeter. This is the long guard. When the sovereign is resident outside London, the guard mounts as a short guard, comprising one corporal of horse, one corporal, and ten troopers.

When the sovereign returns to Buckingham Palace and the Royal Standard is flown above its parapet, the short guard is increased to long guard status by the addition of the missing members described above; this 'make up' rides from Hyde Park Barracks to Horse Guards with covered Standard. The procedure operates in reverse when the sovereign leaves London.

The duty posting of the mounted and dismounted sentries at Horse Guards is decided at the guard inspection carried out at Hyde Park Barracks by the Orderly Officer. The Household Cavalrymen with the most immaculate turnout are allotted the mounted duty: the remainder of the guard is allotted the foot duty over Gate and Guardroom. The latter rotate duty turns over the 24-hour guard period, while the mounted sentries stand guard from 10am to 5pm.

The Guard Mounting at Horse Guards commences with the members of the 'Old Guard' not on duty being paraded in line outside Horse Guards a short period before 11am. If a 'Long Guard' is on duty, the centre of the parade line will be taken by a non-commissioned officer carrying the Standard. The 'Old Guard' officer will command the parade and the trumpeter (both regiments always ride a grey, and wear a red helmet plume) will be to the right of the Guard. The 'New Guard', having ridden down from Hyde Park Barracks, arrives and forms up in parade order to face the 'Old Guard', precisely as Horse Guards' clock strikes 11am. If a 'Long Guard' is changing, the trumpeters of both guards sound the Royal Salute in unison as the 'New Guard' arrives and forms up. Under their respective officer's orders, the two guards formally salute each other, then, the Standard of the 'New Guard' is handed over by the Corporal Major to his Corporal who, in

order to take hold of it in his right hand, first sheathes his sword. The first relief sentries of the 'New Guard' are then led by their Corporal Major into the stable area to exchange duties with the 'Old Guard' sentries currently on duty. During this Guardroom handover, two Troopers from the Old and New Guards patrol in successive pairs between the Guard Mounting and the Guards Memorial, thus fulfilling their ancient duty of guarding the whole Parade Ground precinct. Next, these 'Old Guard' sentries assemble under their Corporal Major and ride out to join the remainder of the 'Old Guard' on parade. The departing Corporal Major takes the Standard from the 'Old Guard' Corporal, who then draws his sword to be in conformity with the rest of the 'Old Guard'. With the trumpeters again sounding the Royal Salute in unison, the 'Old Guard' rides off back to Hyde Park Barracks, following which the remaining members of the 'New Guard' ride into Horse Guards to commence their tour of duty.

An overseas guard mounts at Horse Guards. The Queen's Life Guard found between 28 August–29 September 2000 by a contingent of The Lord Strathcona's Horse (Royal Canadians) during the absence at summer camp of the Household Cavalry. In the last three and a half centuries of this continuous guard, only a very select few other regiments have been accorded the honour of mounting the Sovereign's Life Guard at Horse Guards. A listing of these can be found in Appendix A. (Another Canadian regiment, the Governor General's Horse Guards, has long been affiliated with The Blues and Royals.) (The Household Cavalry Journal)

Horse Guards, though today dwarfed by some of its neighbouring governmental buildings, even in this modern environment continues to retain its own unique place on the shoulders of Whitehall history that centuries of close protective duty both for the Royal Court and also the seat of Parliament, have conferred upon it.

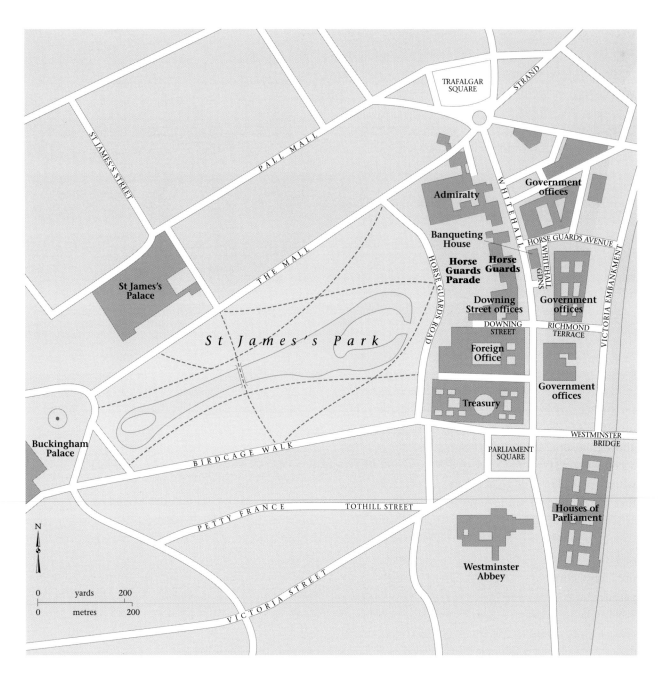

LEFT
Trooping the Colour, pictured in 2005 in perfect sunlight, the King's Troop, Royal Horse Artillery, leads the Household Cavalry past the saluting base. The Colour being Trooped is that of the 1st Battalion, Irish Guards. Only that week the regiment had been the first to receive the battle honour 'IRAQ 2003'. Perhaps uniquely, the Colour Party comprised three brothers, from the Hogan family. (HQ London District)

Where two 'Short Guards' change without the presence of officers, corporal majors, Standards or trumpeters, these parades are commanded by the non-commissioned officers of the Guard and omit the words of command and procedures relevant to the missing guard members. As their availability allows, on some days a Household Cavalry Band will accompany the Guard Change. History was made when on 1 May 2001, Musn. S. Thorpe became the first woman to play trumpet on a Queen's Life Guard at Horse Guards.

At four o'clock each day, the Queen's Life Guard at Horse Guards parades outside the building for a final inspection by the duty officer. This afternoon parade was traditionally connected with an incident in 1894, when the guard on duty failed to turn out and present compliments to Queen Victoria on her passing through the Horse Guards arch. The Monarch then decreed that the Horse Guards' Guard be paraded for inspection by an officer at 4pm every day for the next hundred years: the 'Punishment Parade', as it became known, has obviously served its time, but the observance of tradition has dictated its continuance to the present day.

BELOW
Major-General Roberts presents the Meritorious Service Medal to London District Garrison Sergeant Major W. D. G. Mott, Welsh Guards. The MSM reflects GSM Mott's unique contribution to the distinguished post he holds and recognises how its chivalric values accrued over the centuries have been adapted to modern times through the GSM's concern for the proper courtesy appropriate to each event. At the same time he must ensure that all military events in London district comply with the ever-changing requirements emanating from the MoD building opposite. (Courtesy of The Guards Magazine)

The daily 4 o'clock 'Punishment Parade' at Horse Guards, 1958. The off-duty men from a 'long guard' are seen on parade awaiting the arrival of the Orderly Officer to carry out his inspection. The parade continues today only by tradition: the century of such parades imposed upon the guard by Queen Victoria as a punishment for not turning out as she passed through the arch has now been fulfilled. Formed from The Life Guards regiment, the guard comprises, from the left, a squadron corporal major, trumpeter, corporal, eight troopers, a corporal and two mounted troopers. The author stands fourth from left. (Author's collection)

HORSE GUARDS TODAY

Currently, the senior military officer at Horse Guards is the Major-General Commanding the Household Division. His appointment dates from July 1856, when Lord Rokeby (Scots Guards) was made the first Major-General with special responsibility for the then Brigade of Guards; this posting superseded the previously rotational responsibility of Field Officer-in-Brigade-Waiting. Until 1868, the early office premises of the new Major-General were some rooms in the old Gun House to the north of the parade; and until 1871, the new 'Home District' created by Cardwell was also administered from there. However, after the departure of the Commander-in-Chief from Horse Guards late in 1871, his vacated suite was occupied by the Major-General and his staff to administer the renamed 'London District'; thus it has continued to modern times.[278]

Today, seated in His Grace the Duke of Wellington's old office over the archway, and with the Duke's old desk still *in situ* and in use, the Major-General takes overall supervision of the affairs of both regiments of Household Cavalry – The Life Guards, and The Blues and Royals – and those of the five Foot Guards regiments: Grenadier Guards, Coldstream Guards, Scots Guards, Irish Guards and Welsh Guards. The Major-General may be appointed from any one of these seven regiments. The Major-General's department is also responsible for organizing and carrying out military ceremonies within the capital; this is effected through the Staff Officer Ceremonial together with HM Ceremonial Warrant Officer the Garrison Sergeant Major. Thus it can be seen that this modern ceremonial role of Horse Guards represents a clear line of descent from the court department of Queen Elizabeth I's Champion at Tilt, Sir Henry Lee, discussed in the opening chapters of this

narrative; for many decades, he organized the Whitehall Tiltyard Tudor tournaments on the Horse Guards' site.

In respect of ceremonial, all such modern events derive from fact; original serious purposes underpin the displays of traditions for which Horse Guards has become a synonym. That London military ceremony appears to observers as a study in perfection is due in large part to the seemingly limitless expertise and experience, displayed with incomparable authority, by the London District Garrison Sergeant Major (GSM). At the time of writing, there have been eight GSMs since 1940, and each has maintained, and endeavoured to

The King's Troop, Royal Horse Artillery, assumes Horse Guards duty. For some years now it has been a settled routine for the King's Troop RHA to take the Queen's Life Guard when the Household Cavalry is out of London at summer camp. During the latter three or so weeks, the Household Cavalry horses and men enjoy an extended break in the country: a period of great benefit to both horses and riders. Depicted is a Life Guards guard handing over to the King's Troop. (Media Operations, HQ London District)

The eternal guard. This most evocative view of The Queen's Life Guard leaving Horse Guards in the snows of winter conceals a much more sinister event. On the day prior to this photo in 1991, the IRA had attempted a mortar attack on 10 Downing Street from a van parked off Horse Guards Avenue, one result of which was some panes of the Major-General's window being blown in. They are seen in the photo as the ones boarded. The Queen's Life Guard routine was not interrupted. (Courtesy of The Guards Magazine)

Sir Henry Lee was pleased to hear the event was deemed to be 'a superb reconstruction of ancient chivalry'. Six combatant knights participated in the indoor evening jousting tournament, accompanied by appropriate music from the band of the 2nd Life Guards. His Grace the Duke of Marlborough, competing in an armour of 'dark steel etched with gold', was deemed Champion at Tilt and received a solid gold cup worth £600 from 'the Queen of Beauty', Lady Curzon.[280]

Also at Horse Guards, supporting the department of the Major-General, are two regimental headquarters teams – one for Household Cavalry matters, and the other for Foot Guards matters. The Commander Household Cavalry (Silver Stick-in-Waiting) exercises authority through his RHQ departmental staff for the former, over all their home and overseas stations. With regard to Foot Guards' affairs, the Lieutenant Colonel Foot Guards, with his RHQ staff, takes responsibility for his five regiments across all their home and worldwide commitments.

Sharing the building with all these regimental offices will be the new Household Cavalry Museum. Here, visitors can study the story of Horse Guards, the lives of its attendant military and civilian staffs and its historical links to old and new Whitehall.

So, as it has done so for centuries, Horse Guards continues to protect the most historic site in Whitehall. Should the ghosts of Horse Guards' history take a walk past the building today, both Henry VIII and Elizabeth I might offer a knowing nod to the armoured sentries, recalling their tournament knights fighting to be Champion at Tilt; Jacobean architect Inigo Jones would look approvingly on Horse Guards' tooled stonework, pleased with Kent's

surpass, the standards of his predecessor: none has ever fallen short, equally in displays of both celebration and mourning.[279] The incumbent of the post in July 1912, however, would have faced an ultimate challenge if perhaps he was asked to advise on the re-enactment of a full Tudor military tournament at Earls Court before Queen Alexandra. Whether he was so asked remains unrecorded, but no doubt the ghost of

The heartbeat of London. Turn by turn, day by day, year in year out (give or take a couple of world wars), for three and half centuries the Household Cavalry guard has ridden away from Horse Guards in London after handing over the duty of Sovereign's Life Guard to the New Guard for the next 24 hours. The scene here, depicting The Life Guards' guard riding back to Hyde Park Barracks, is as unchanging and predictable as the rotation of the seasons. This guard-changing ceremony and the Horse Guards sentries in Whitehall – at whom everyone who passes by takes a look – is an embedded feature of London's city psyche. Its citizens expect it always to remain so in their lifetimes.
(Country Life)

efforts to emulate his style; Cromwell's keen eye would note the military accoutrements, not least the blue tunics, akin to his New Model; likewise, the Merry Monarch, with Monck at his side, would see the guard as a ready escort; the Georgian War Office civil servants might hurry into their archway office entrances seeing nothing amiss. The only disappointed visitors from times past could be those looking in vain for their favourite coffee house corner table. Otherwise, little might appear to have changed over the passage of all those years. But clear evidence is available to the visitor of today to show that the Horse Guards sentries are very much more than presenters of tradition: the display of medals worn by many of them is a sombre testimony that since the Second World War there has only been one year (1968) in which no English serviceman or servicewoman has died in conflict. In all the conflicts of the other years, there has been some representation of either the Household Cavalry, or the Foot Guards, or both. Wherever these regiments have served, Horse Guards has always exercised a benign influence on their well-being; it is to be hoped that it will forever continue in that role.

Appendices

APPENDIX A
Other regiments furnishing the Sovereign's Life Guard at Horse Guards

Although this is an area still requiring further research, it is possible to list at least the following documented occasions when regiments other than the Household Cavalry have performed the duty of Sovereign's Life Guard at Horse Guards.

January 1689–November 1697
The Dutch 'Blue' Guards

Following the flight of James II, the new king, William III, disbanded the Horse Guards' predominantly Catholic Fourth Troop, replacing it on the English establishment with a troop of his own Dutch 'Blue' Guards. Dispersing the other English Horse Guards troops to various rural postings, he entrusted the Horse Guards' guard to his own Dutch soldiers. For at least one unhappy consequence of this change see p.62 above.

12 June 1731
General Wade's Horse, or 3rd Dragoon Guards

The 3rd Dragoon Guards were reported in the *Country Journal* of this date, the reason being that the Horse Guards were all attending a review in Hyde Park. Major-General George Wade (1673–1748) had been C-in-C of Scotland since 1726 and was making his name as a pre-eminent military road architect and map-maker in partnership with William Roy, Deputy Quartermaster General of Scotland. Their joint efforts led to the foundation of the Ordnance Survey in 1791. The choice of his regiment for this prestigious duty was perhaps due to his leading part in foiling a West Country Jacobite coup against the king in 1715. The 3rd Dragoon Guards are today amalgamated within The Royal Scots Dragoon Guards (Carabiniers and Greys).

4 June 1763
15th Light Dragoons

'On Lord Granby's welcome home in February 1763, he was warmly welcomed by his sovereign, who further favoured the distinguished soldier, at the great Hyde Park review held on 4 June, by according him the post of honour. On this occasion the Fifteenth took the King's duty – a compliment well earned by their brilliant achievements during the war.'[281] The 15th Light Dragoons are today 15th/19th King's Royal Hussars.

26 June 1765
The Royal Regiment of Horse Guards (Blue)

According to Sir George Arthur in his *The Story of the Household Cavalry*, on this date, 'In point of fact, the Blues performed the King's duty...'[282]

25 May 1776
The Royal Regiment of Horse Guards (Blue)

'Gen.Conway is asked by the Commr.-in.Chief if the Blues would like to take temporary duty at the Whitehall guard.'[283]

25 May 1788–4 June 1789
The Royal Regiment of Horse Guards (Blue)

The Blues and Royals today share the duty at Horse Guards equally with The Life Guards, but they were only formally granted full Household Cavalry status in June 1820. Consequently, during this appearance at Horse Guards in the 1780s for the duration of the reorganization of the Life Guards Troops, they were still only recognized as a non-Household Cavalry horsed regiment.[284]

6 July 1815
14th Light Dragoons, The London and Westminster Light Horse Volunteers

This marked the only time so far known when a Yeomanry regiment furnished the Sovereign's Life Guard at Horse Guards. At the Public Record Office, dated as above, can be found the following order from the C-in-C's office to Lieutenant Colonel Baker, commanding the 14th Light Dragoons:

Sir... I have received the Comd. in Chief's Commands to acquaint you, that the London and Westminster Light Horse Volunteers will on Thursday next the 13th inst., achieve and continue to furnish until further Orders, the King's Guard at the Horse Guards, at present taken by the 14th Light Dragoons. I have in consequence to request that you will take an early opportunity of communicating with Colonel Herries of the London and Westminster Light Horse Volunteers, and furnish him with a detail of the Guard, with a Copy of these instructions as necessary for the guidance of the Corps on the above Duty.[285]

The Household Cavalry regiments were, of course, otherwise engaged at Waterloo. On return from the Continent, they resumed Horse Guards' duty in February 1816, having initially relinquished it on 3 May 1815. The 14th Light Dragoons became the 14th/20th King's Hussars, while the London and Westminster Light Horse Volunteers became part of the Inns of Court & County of London Yeomanry, today the Household Cavalry's Territorial Army unit.

1822
9th Lancers

As quoted in his *A Short History of The Life Guards*, R. J. T. Hills says, 'the Household Cavalry were commonly relieved whenever they were to function at a review, certainly as early as 1822, when the 9th Lancers took the guard for a day, coming under the orders of the Gold Stick for the purpose'.[286] The 9th Lancers became the 9th/12th Lancers in 1960.

July 1823
The Royal Dragoons

'For two weeks in July 1823 the Royals occupied the Regent's Park cavalry barracks to take over 'King's Duty' in London in lieu of the Household Cavalry, who went to Hounslow for a big review.'[287] The Royal Dragoons are today The Blues and Royals.

August 1832
The Royal Dragoons

'In autumn the Royals went to London in relief of the Life Guards.'[288] This duty relates to the presentation of new Standards to the Royal Horse Guards which took place on Queen Adelaide's birthday (13 August) at

Windsor Castle.[289] In the Museum of London there is a painting by James Holland of this date depicting, in the middle distance, a unit of undefined Line cavalry processing south through Constitution Arch, perhaps the Royals going from Hyde Park Barracks to Horse Guards.

June 1913
19th Hussars

The Household Cavalry was attending a royal review in Windsor Great Park in front of George V. The King wished to recreate the summer event of 1880 when Queen Victoria made her eldest son, Edward, Colonel-in-Chief of the Household Cavalry. The culmination of the review was a charge of both regiments across the Park of which a breathless *Times* correspondent reported, 'The gallop had been nothing to this ... it was something of a relief when they pulled up ... the long line still beautifully and mathematically straight, the onlookers still untrampled!'[290] The 19th Hussars are today the 15th/19th The King's Royal Hussars.

1973 et seq.
The King's Troop Royal Horse Artillery

Up to 1973, each of the two Household Cavalry mounted squadrons (The Life Guards and The Blues & Royals) left London in turn to enjoy, horses and men, summer camp under canvas in the rural environment of the Home Counties. One squadron provided all the Horse Guards duty while the other was away. In 1973, it was decided that henceforth both squadrons should go to camp at the same time; for the duration of the camp, usually three weeks, the Queen's Life Guard was entrusted to The King's Troop Royal Horse Artillery. The King's Troop outranks the Household Cavalry in army seniority only when it is on parade with its guns, as seen in current Queen's Birthday Parades where the King's Troop, with its field guns (which are its Colours), forms up to the right of the Household Cavalry. This precedence has its origins in an order to all the Royal Horse Artillery from the Duke of Cambridge in 1857, but subsequently amended to apply only when 'on parade, with their guns' (see p.127).

8–23 September 2000
The Lord Strathcona's Horse (Royal Canadians)

An account of the events of this goodwill visit by 18 members of this affiliated colonial regiment occurs in *The Household Cavalry Journal* 2000/01. The following extracts are reproduced by kind permission of the editor:

The Household Cavalry Mounted Regiment hosted 18 members of the Lord Strathcona's Horse from the 28 August to 29 September 2000. The purpose of their visit was to carry out 7 Queen's Life Guards [QLG] at Horse Guards... On 30 August each Lord Strathcona soldier was issued with his Cavalry horse and army tack. Corporal of Horse Jenkins RHG/D, then spent 8 days teaching them the intricacies of QLG. Their first guard was on the 8th September ... the 12th September saw them start QLG, they were on every other day until the 22 September. On Saturday 23 September the Lord Strathcona's rode off QLG for the last time, handed the horses and tack back over to the Squadrons... The conclusion of the visit was that it went extremely well.

APPENDIX B
War Office Staff at Horse Guards in 1782

The following list was drawn up by Secretary-at-War Charles Jenkinson. The text is included in full:

Account of the Persons employ'd in the War Office, their Business, Salaries and Perquisites

The Secretary at War: His Salary is £2476 p Ann clear. He receives no Fees whatever, except on the Renewal of Commissions at the Demise of the Crown. He has the whole Direction under the King of the Department of War, and appoints the Under Secretary and all other Principal & Supernumary Clerks, Messengers & other Persons employ'd in the Office.

The Several Persons at present employ'd in the Office are as follows Viz.

Deputy Secretary at War, M. Lewis Esq.: His salary is £320 p Ann but he is entitled to Fees arising from the Entry of Commissions. This makes his Place to be worth £500 p Ann in Time of Peace and £900 p Ann in Time of War. And he has also a Contingent Warrant for £200 p Ann. more during the Time of the Militia being called out.

First Clerk, M. Lewis Esq.: His salary is £100 p Ann but he is entitled to Fees which make this Place worth £800 p Ann in Time of Peace and £2000 in Time of War. He has the Care of the Detail of the General Business of the Office and superintends the Conduct of all the Clerks.

Principal Clerk and Examiner of Army Accts., R. Taylor Esq.: His salary is £520 p Ann with a certain Share of Fees which makes his Place worth £630 p Ann in Time of Peace and about £750 in Time of War. He also receives a Moiety of the Emoluments of the Deputy Secretary. The whole Department of Accounts is under his Control nor is he considered as subject to the Directions of the Deputy Secretary, as the other Clerks are but only of the Secretary at War himself.

Principal Clerk Assist. To the Examiner of Army Accts., Mr. Collings: His Salary is £200 p Ann besides which he is entitled to Fees on attested Copies of the Beating Orders – which Fees amount to about £120 p Ann in Time of Peace and £250 in Time of War.

Secretary & Clerk established, Mr. Merry: His Salary is £200 p Ann by means of the following arrangement. The late Clerk examinant has retired with the King's leave retaining £300 p Ann of his salary from Midsummer 1782. The remainder of his Salary is given to Mr. Taylor who succeeds him retaining his former Salary as Assistant but giving up his Fees on Beating Orders as follows viz: Mr. Collings succeeding to the Office as Assistant to Mr. Taylor engages to pay to the Private Secretary £125 p Ann out of the Fees for Beating Orders, and £25 p Ann to Mr. Plenderleith now Assistant to Mr. Marsh. The remainder he takes as his salary – on Condition that if the Surplus fall short of £50 it shall be made good to him out of the Contingent Office Bills – So that the Salary of the Private Secretary will be as follows £73-10-0 as Clerk in the Room of Mr. Collings £21 as Attendant on the Secretary at War and £125 to be paid by Mr. Collings out of the Fees for Beating Orders. In all

£200 p Ann until some better Provision can be made for the Private Secretary.

Principal Clerk, Mr. Marsh: Salary £110 p Ann with Fees which make the Place worth £600 p Ann in Time of Peace and as far as £1500 p Ann in Time of War and he has at Present the apartments of the Deputy at War with Coals and Candles. He is responsible for the Estimates & Establishments – Collects the returns of the Garrisons & of the Staff at Home and Abroad & prepares Warrants for their Payment. Furnishes the secretary at War with Lists of Quarters and assists the First Clerk in directing the Current business of the Office. He has been in the Office ever since 1759.

Principal Clerk, Mr. Leece: He is the Oldest Clerk in the Office. His salary is £90 p Ann. His Fees are the same as Mr. Marsh's, consequently his Place is of the same Value. His business is to superintend the Letter writers Desk to take an Account of & receive the Fees upon the Several warrants & to administer the oaths to Widows & Officers which he does *Gratis*.

Principal Clerk, Mr. Morse: His salary is £80 p Ann with Fees on the Entry of Commissions & on Warrants for Courts Martial which makes his Place worth about £300 p Ann besides which he has an allowance of £100 p Ann for compiling the List of the Army & he has all the Profits of Printing it. He has also £100 for his trouble in keeping a Book for the king containing a register of the Services of the Several Officers of the Army another £100 for extra Clerks employed by him in Entering the several Changes & Additions to the King's Book. His business is to take and Enter Commissions and to receive the Deputy Secretary at War's fees

upon them & a small Fee for himself. The deputy Secretary Fee's on Commissions are one Day's Pay according to the Rank of the Commission. He has been in the Office ever since the year 1753.

Established Clerk, Mr. Channing: Has been in the office ever since 1756. His salary is £110 and Fees to the Amount of about £50 p Ann more for Keeping the Account of Expences on Deserters sent from their several Establishments.

Anor.Clerk Established, Mr. Davies: His salary is £110 p Ann with £20 allow'd him by the First Clerk for paying Allowances on the Compassionate List. He likewise pays the Widows of the Army under the appointment of the Paymaster of the Widows Pensions (Mr. H. Fox).

Anor.Clerk Established, Mr. Clinton: His salary is £120 p Ann. He was Private Secretary to Mr. Barrington & has obtained an Additional salary of £100 till better provided for. His business is to make out the Contingent Bills of the Office and to receive the salary for the Secretary at War. He also keeps an Index of the Business of the Office arranged according to the several regiments which is called the Journal Book.

Anor.Clerk Established, Mr. Clements: His Salary is £154-12-0. He writes the Notifications & takes Charge of all the Papers relating to them. Registers the Leaves of Absence & Publishes Promotions in the Gazette.

Anor.Clerk Established, Mr. Bowles: His salary is £150. He writes in the Deputy Secretary's Room endorses & Keeps all his Papers.

Anor.Clerk Established, Mr. Weir: His salary is £73-10-0. He keeps an Account of Compassionate cases which with copying papers & Letters gives him full employment.

Anor.Clerk Established, Mr. Plenderleith: His salary is £100 p Ann. He is Assistant to Mr. Marsh in the Estimates Business & in the Accounts of the establishments.

There are also six Supernumary Clerks, whose salaries are as follows, viz.

Mr. Dodd and Mr. Green, at £100 p Ann Each

Mr. Watkins and [space blank], at £73-10-0 p Ann Each

Mr. Winder and Mr. W. Mackay, at £52-10-0 p Ann Each

Their Business is to Transcribe, Copy and Enter all Letters & Orders into the Books of the Office which is done very regularly. The Senior of these (Mr. Dodd) also keeps the Account & has the Care of all Correspondence relating to Deserters. Mr. Mackay has also £52-10-0 p Ann for preparing all the Books of Returns & is frequently employed on *extra* Business for which he has *extra* Pay allowed him when employ'd.

Office Keepers:

Mr. Green at £100 Profits included; Mrs Green at £30 p Ann do.

Establish'd Messenger, Mr. Stacey: Salary £60 p Ann.

Acting Messenger, Mr. George Doyle: worth about £150 p Ann.

Assistant Messenger, Mr. Jas. Harrington: salary £10 p Ann & Wages of 12s p Week

Two Porters: at 12s P Week wages

20 July 1782[291]

Certainly a job in Georgian army administration was worth hanging on to. Of these staff listed Harman Leece served some 50 years, Charles Marsh 35 years, Andrew Clinton 40 years, and Charles Plenderleith 30 years. Matthew Lewis, we see, is holding down the two most senior (and lucrative) office posts at the same time. He was Deputy Secretary-at-War from 1775 to 1803.

Leonard Moore, starting at the bottom as a Clerk in 1757, also found time in a career which extended to 1807 to achieve a Fellowship of the Royal Society. Mr Bowles lived in an attic apartment over the Secretary-at-War's chambers.[292] Mr Collings' 'Beating Orders' fees refers to recruitment by drum-beat, where itinerant recruiting teams advertised their presence to likely volunteers by beating drums on the march in the chosen locality.[293] As for 'Mr Mackay' with his undefined 'extra business' and its 'extra pay', might he have had family ties with the C-in-C Scotland Lieutenant General the Honourable Alexander Mackay that enabled him to undertake sensitive assignments as occasion required?

In respect of copying and recording correspondence, typically each and every War Office paper of significance was subject to the following process – drafting, copying, examining, despatching and entering. As the War Office expanded in Victorian times so complete individual departments were set up to control each of these stages of documentary production.

The tradition for service longevity at Horse Guards continues unabated to the present day. In the year 2000 two lady members of the Civil Service staff completed respectively 50 years and 37 years continuous service there. Their contribution to the smooth running of the military posts at the highest level was recognized with the award of respectively, membership of the Royal Victorian Order (MVO) and an Imperial Service Medal (ISM); and an MBE.

Endnotes

1.   PRO CVA 1519.
2.   E. Hall (ed. Willis), *Chronicle* (1809), p.786. See also L&P H.VIII, Sept. 1531, p.201, f.408, for fuller details of the Horse Guards site transferring from private to Crown ownership at this date.
3.   G. Rosser, *Medieval Westminster 1200–1540* (Clarendon, 1989), passim.
4.   LCC, *Survey of London*, Vol. XIII, p.19. See also S. Thurley, *Royal Palaces of Tudor England* (Paul Mellon Center BA, 1993).
5.   Viscount Dillon, 'Armour Notes', *Archaeological Journal*, 1903, pp.59–62.
6.   Hall, *Chronicle*.
7.   A. Young, *Tudor and Jacobean Tournaments* (George Philip, 1987) for an excellent modern account of the often misunderstood world of the armoured knight. For jousting cheques specifically, vide C. J. Ffoulkes, 'Jousting cheques of the sixteenth century', *Archeologia* Vol.LXIII.
8.   HMC, *Rutland* IV p.499.
9.   J. Bruce (ed.), *The Diary of John Manningham* (Camden Society, 1868), 19 March 1601.
10. S. Pepys, *The Diary*, 11 vols (HarperCollins, 2000), 22 June 1660.
11. C. Wriothesley (ed. W. D. Hamilton), *Chronicle of England 1485–1559* (Camden Society), NS 11, 20.
12. L&P H.VIII, VI, no.1112.
13. Wroithesley, *Chronicle of England*.
14. British Library, Mss.Cotton Vesp. C.i.177, for a letter from Lord Berners, ambassador in Spain, describing the sport.
15. J. G. Nichols (ed.), *The Diary of Henry Machyn 1550–1563* (Camden Society, 1848).
16. *Royal Historical Society Transactions*, 2nd Series, IX, p.236.
17. E. Lodge, *Illustrations of British History* (edn. II, 1838), pp.97–8.
18. Nichols, *Diary of Henry Machyn*.
19. HMC, *Rutland*, 14 May 1571.
20. General Sir M. Gow, *Trooping the Colour* (Souvenir Press, 1989) gives the best modern and most comprehensive account of this unique traditional ceremony.
21. *Londina Illustra*, 17 November 1581.
22. A. Young, *Tudor and Jacobean Tournaments*, p.56.
23. H. Goldwell, *A briefe declaration of the shews* (1581).
24. HMC, *Salisbury* XV, 1 April 1603.
25. LCC, *Survey of London*, Vol. XIII, Part 2, p.7.
26. G. P. V. Akrigg, *Jacobean Pageant* (Athenaeum, 1972), p.158.
27. R. Strong, *Henry, Prince of Wales* (Thames & Hudson 1986), pp.64–6.
28. See 'Mr. Sidney Lee', *The Times*, 27 December 1905.
29. PRO E 351/3256.
30. J. Harington, *Nugae Antiquae* (London 1804), pp.349–52.
31. British Library, Add.Mss. 6297, f.185.
32. J. A. Gotch, 'The Original Drawings for a Palace at Whitehall, attributed to Inigo Jones', *Architectural Review*, June 1912; see also M. Whinney, 'John Webb's drawings for Whitehall Palace', *Walpole Society* XXXI, 1946.
33. Westminster Abbey Muniments, 2 February 1626.
34. PRO CSP Dom. Charles I, CCCCLI, April 1640.
35. PRO LC 5/135.
36. PRO CSP Dom. Charles I, CCCCLXXXVI.
37. HMC, *Montagu*, 30 December 1641.
38. E. Hockliffe (ed.), *The Diary of the Rev. Ralph Josselin 1616–1683* (Camden Society 3rd Ser. XV, 1908).
39. W. Lithgow, *The Present Svrveigh of London and Englands State* (printed O. U., 1643).
40. House of Commons Journals, 16 July 1645.
41. Pepys, *The Diary*, 13 October 1660.
42. PRO CSP Dom. 1649–50, 4 August 1649.
43. Ibid., p.240.
44. Ibid., p.551.
45. G. Berry, *Seventeenth Century England: Traders and Their Tokens* (Seaby, 1988), passim.
46. Sir R. Strong, *Lost Treasures of Britain* (Viking, 1990), p.111.
47. PRO LR 2/124 Inventory of Charles I's possessions intended for sale; PRO SP 28/282–285 Inventory of Whitehall Palace goods intended for sale 1649–1658.
48. PRO CSP Dom. 4 September 1651.
49. N. Sjoberg (ed.), *Johan Ekeblads bref* (Stockholm 1911), p.411.
50. E. S. De Beer (ed.), *The Diary of John Evelyn* (Oxford University Press, 1959), 11 January 1656.
51. Sir William Dugdale, *A Short View of the Late Troubles, etc* (Oxford, 1681).
52. *Mercurius Politicus*, July 1654.
53. L. Hotson, *The Commonwealth and Restoration Stage* (Cambridge Mass., 1928), p.44.
54. PRO CSP Dom. 1656–57.
55. A. Bryant, *King Charles II* (Collins, 1960), p.79.
56. Pepys, *The Diary*, 3 February 1660.
57. G. Davies, *The Early History of the Coldstream Guards* (Oxford, 1924), p.103
58. *Mercurius Publicus*, 8–15 November 1660, for details of an extraordinary official furnishings presentation of a crimson velvet bedroom furniture suite.
59. Pepys, *The Diary*, 20 March 1660.
60. PRO CVA.
61. Pepys, *The Diary*.
62. G. Davies, *The Early History of the Coldstream Guards*, p.111.
63. PRO WORK 5/2.
64. Ibid.
65. B. Lillywhite, *London Coffee Houses. A reference book of coffee houses of the seventeenth, eighteenth and nineteenth centuries* (George Allen and Unwin, 1965).
66. PRO CSPD 1664–5.
67. Pepys, *The Diary*, 27 November 1662.
68. Ibid.
69. Ibid., 1 January 1663.
70. D. Ascoli, *A Companion to the British Army 1660–1983* (Harrap, 1983), p.19.

71. PRO WORK 5/4.
72. PRO WORK 5/5 & 5/6; see also some (incomplete) accounts ledgers in Worcester College, Oxford.
73. De Beer, *Diary of John Evelyn*, 19 October 1661.
74. PRO WORK 5/4.
75. Ibid.
76. Ibid.
77. Ibid.
78. British Library, King's Mss. E. XVII.12, 19 December 1644 describes the sentencing of a trooper of William Waller's regiment to ride the wooden horse. An illustration of this instrument of punishment is in F. Grose, *Military Antiquities respecting a History of the English Army*, 2 vols (London, 1812), Vol. II, p.106.
79. PRO WAR 89/1, General Courts Martial 1666–95.
80. D. Mackinnon, *Origin and Services of the Coldstream Guards*, 2 vols (London, 1833), p.326.
81. PRO WAR 72/56, p.1; WAR 81/69, p.73.
82. Captain Sir George Arthur, *The Story of the Household Cavalry*, 3 vols (Vols I and II: Constable, 1909; (Vol. III: Heinemann, 1926), Vol. I, p.35 n.
83. Ibid., Vol. I, pp.35–6.
84. PRO CSP Dom. Charles II 1676–7, p.342, 28 September 1676.
85. PRO LC 5/202 pp.210–12. I am indebted to horologist Oliver Harris for calling my attention to this entry.
86. PRO CSP Dom. Charles II 1663–4, 6 April 1664.
87. Pepys, *The Diary*, 26 August 1664.
88. *The Times Picture Collection – London* (Harper Collins 2001), p.94.
89. PRO CSP Dom Charles II 1660–70.
90. HMC, *F. W. Leybourne-Popham*, Vol.I, p.275.
91. N. Luttrell, *Brief Historical Relation of State Affairs* (1857), Vol.2, p.212.
92. T. Gumble, *The Life of General Monck, Duke of Albemarle* (London, 1671).
93. PRO CSPD 1664–5 p.214, Gumble, *The Life of General Monck*, p.236.
94. Pepys, *The Diary*, 20 June 1665.
95. PRO CSPD 1664–5, p.492.
96. Arthur, *The Story of the Household Cavalry*, Vol.I, p.70.
97. Pepys, *The Diary*, 22 February 1664 '…and which is worst of all, that he [Charles II] will alter the present militia and bring all to a flying army.'
98. Pepys, *The Diary*, Companion Vol. X, pp.13–14.
99. Ibid.
100. Ibid.
101. Ibid.
102. Ibid.
103. Ibid., 24 March 1668. Lord Brouncker, a naval Commissioner, shared musical interests with Pepys.
104. Ibid., 9 November 1666.
105. Ibid., 23 January 1667.
106. An aquatint by W. H. Pyne of 1805 depicts the event. The Lottery Office storing the wheel was on the south side of the Banqueting House, under the visual security of the Horse Guards guards. See also LCC, *Survey of London*, Vol. XIII, pp.221–222.
107. De Beer, *Diary of John Evelyn*
108. Ibid., Addenda, p.589.
109. PRO WAR 26/2, 1673.
110. PRO WAR 71/13–33 for general courts martial held at Horse Guards.
111. PRO WAR 71/1– 12 for Board of General Officers proceedings.
112. PRO WAR 26/2, pp.342–3.
113. PRO WORK 5/15, December 1670.
114. De Beer, *Diary of John Evelyn*, op.cit., 29 June 1678.
115. PRO CTB 1685–9 Vol. III, p.1819, 19 March 1687; and Vol.IV, p.1969, 26 June 1688.
116. Arthur, *The Story of the Household Cavalry*, Vol. I, p.116.
117. PRO CTB 7 January 1679.
118. PRO WAR Warrants 55/424.
119. PRO WAR Ordnance 47/12, f.33.
120. PRO WAR Ordnance 47/12, f.70.
121. *Wren Society* Court Orders, 8 November 1693.
122. PRO CTB VII, Pt. I, pp.135–6.
123. N. Pevsner, *The Cities of London and Westminster* (Penguin, 1973), p.549. Subsequent editions omit this tradition.
124. British Library, Add.Mss. 9, 727–8 being two volumes of letters from officers about movement, quartering, and recruiting and miscellaneous personal matters over some 20 years. Further papers are with Gloucestershire CRO under ref. D 1799. See also G. A. Jacobsen, *William Blathwayt, A Late Seventeenth Century Administrator* (London and New Haven, 1932).
125. The original manuscript is held at the PRO under ref. WAR 30/48.
126. De Beer, *Diary of John Evelyn*, 6 February 1685.
127. Ibid., 7 February 1685.
128. HMC, *F. W. Leybourne-Popham*, Vol. I, 1685, p.265.
129. Arthur, *The Story of the Household Cavalry*, Vol. I, p.230.
130. Ibid., p.234.
131. vide NAM, Binns Collection, *The Life Guards*. p.2.
132. PRO CTB 1689–92, I, 23 September 1689, p.263.
133. For the role of Captain Sylver in demolishing houses for firebreaks, see Brigadier O. F. G. Hogg 'The Office of Master Gunner of Whitehall and St. James's Park', *Journal of the Royal Artillery*, 1978 Vol CV, Pt.2, p.87.
134. De Beer, *Diary of John Evelyn*, op.cit., 10 April 1691.
135. *Post Boy*, 18 November 1697.
136. De Beer, *Diary of John Evelyn*, op.cit., 4 January 1698.
137. HMC, *F. W. Rawdon Hastings*, Vol. II.
138. Wren Society, *Parentalia*.
139. Ibid. The 'grenadiers' mentioned were from the Horse Grenadier Troop attached to the Horse Guards from 1678.
140. Luttrell, *Brief Historical Relation*, Vol. IV, p.239.
141. See also British Library, Add.Mss. 32504 f.54 and the *Flying Post*, or *Postmaster* No. 414, 5 January 1698, and 17–19 February 1698.
142. Luttrell, *Brief Historical Relation*, 8 November 1698, 'The Banquetting House is fitting up for a Chappel'.
143. PRO WORK 38/229 for architectural detail. For access apply to D of E, Dept. DHEM/A1; see also *Archaelogia*,Vol. 25, January 1832 for an account by the architect Sydney Smirke.

144. PRO LRRO 1/484 (MPE 325), 1670 Survey of Whitehall by. J. Fisher, eng. G. Vertue 1747.
145. PRO CSP Dom. July–December 1695, 21 February 1695, p.312.
146. PRO CTP 1708–14, p.66.
147. PRO CTP 1557–1696, 9 October 1695, p.465.
148. PRO CSP Dom. 1696, 10 September 1696, p.381.
149. PRO CTB 1698, 18 November 1697, p.157.
150. PRO Treasury Warrants XVI, 4 April 1699, pp.271–2.
151. PRO CTB 1689–92, II, pp.980–1, 14 January 1691.
152. PRO CTP 1708–14, p.298, 13 August 1711.
153. *London Gazette*, 30 October 1679.
154. House of Lords Journals XVIII, 10 February 1707.
155. *Protestant Loyalty Fairly Drawn* (1681), see also British Library, Add.Mss. 34, 362, f.52, 'On the Coffee Houses'.
156. F. B. Weiner, *Civilians under Military Justice* (Chicago, 1967), p.16.
157. PRO CTB 1696–97, p.181.
158. C. Jones and G. Holmes (eds.), *The London Diaries of William Nicolson, Bishop of Carlisle 1702–1718* (Clarendon Press, 1985), p.266.
159. Arthur, *The Story of the Household Cavalry*, Vol. 1, p.311.
160. The *Weekly Intelligencer*, 14 November 1727.
161. D. Defoe, *The Storm* (1704), Guildhall Library A.8.4.No.6.
162. PRO WORK 6/14, f.83.
163. Ibid., f.176.
164. PRO WORK 6/5, 30 August 1710.
165. PRO Treasury Papers T1/159/12.
166. Arthur, *The Story of the Household Cavalry*, Vol. I, p.328 n.
167. PRO WORK, 23 April 1718 & 31 April 1718.
168. PRO CTB 1718 II, 30 September 1718, p.573.
169. See *London: Whitehall and the Privy Garden* by Canaletto of 1747 showing these alterations, and the guard.
170. PRO LC 5/160.
171. M. Jourdain, *The Work of William Kent* (Country Life, 1948).
172. PRO CTP October 1733.
173. PRO T 52/37–8.
174. PRO T 56/19, p.38.
175. *The Diary of Joseph Farington 1747–1821*, 16 vols (Yale University Press, 1984), Vol. XIV, p.5065.
176. CSP Dom. 36/39, f.116.
177. The *Daily Intelligencer*, 1736.
178. W. G. Constable (rev. J. G. Links), *Canaletto*, 2 vols (Oxford, 1976).
179. Sir M. Gow, *Trooping the Colour* (Souvenir Press, 1988), p.17.
180. PRO WAR 4/40, p.312.
181. PRO WORK 6/17, p.4 & CTB 1743–45, p.770.
182. *Gentlemen's Magazine*, April 1747.
183. PRO WORK 6/63.
184. PRO WORK 6/17, f.57.
185. PRO WAR 26/21, 2 September 1749.
186. PRO T 29/31, p.276.
187. PRO WORK 6/64, 28 February 1754.
188. Ibid., 7 April 1756.
189. Ibid., November 1753–June 1760.
190. PRO WORK 6/63–64 1750–1760, and RIBA refs. HOR/1/1, HOR/1/2, HOR/1/3, HOR/1/4.
191. PRO T 54/26, pp.27, 85.
192. J. Uglow, *Hogarth: A Life and a World* (Faber, 1997), p.34.
193. Jourdain, *The Work of William Kent*, pp.49–50.
194. PRO WORK 6/63.
195. Ibid.
196. PRO WORK 6/64.
197. LCC, *Survey of London*, Vol. XVI, p.14 n.
198. Pepys, *The Diary*, 27 Nov 1660.
199. PRO WAR 26/23, p.333.
200. A. Valentine, *Lord George Germain* (Clarendon Press, 1962).
201. *London Chronicle*.
202. *The Royal Mews* (Pitkin Pictorials Ltd, 1964), p.5.
203. PRO HO 936 31 March–30 June 1768, p.356.
204. Boswell to Hon. Andrew Erskine, 16 Feb 1762.
205. MacKinnon, *Origin and Services*, June 1770.
206. *Bemerkungen eines Reisenden durch England* (Altenberg, 1775), p.416.
207. John Wilmot, Earl of Rochester, *A Ramble in St. James's Park* (1672).
208. *The Gazetteer*, 21 June 1766.
209. H. von Erffa & A. Staley, *The Paintings of Benjamin West* (Yale University Press, 1986), p.418.
210. Jones and Holmes, *The London Diaries of William Nicolson*, p.416.
211. See also H. Mayhew (ed. P. Quennell), *Mayhew's London* (Spring Books, 1st pub. 1851), pp.127–8.
212. Mrs Orford's memoirs in *The Confectioners Union*, December 1922, January–March 1923 (British Library P.P.1423.lct).
213. PRO WORK 16/27/10, pp.121–160 Correspondence; ibid., 16/27/11 The Petition.
214. *Wren Society* Vol. XVIII, p.61, 30 Sep 1686.
215. PRO SP 44/142, p.437.
216. Arthur, *The Story of the Household Cavalry*, Vol. II, p.480.
217. Ibid., p.481.
218. Ibid., p.490.
219. United Grand Lodge of England, Freemasons' Hall, London WC.
220. Parliamentary Papers 1812–13, pp.478, 512 and PRO WAR 4/189, p.155.
221. Gold Stick Orders 1803, Household Cavalry Museum.
222. Mackinnon, *Origin and Services*, 13 June 1735.
223. R. J. T. Hills, *Famous Regiments – The Life Guards* (Leo Cooper, 1971), p.76.
224. SQMC R. J. T. Hills, *A Short History of The Life Guards* (Gale & Polden, 1933), pp.56–7.
225. Arthur, *The Story of the Household Cavalry*, Vol. 2, p.532.
226. Ibid., Vol.2, p.628.
227. C. Dupin, *History and State of the Military Force of Great Britain*, 2 vols (John Murray, 1822).
228. J. &. D. A. Darling, *The Horse Guards by the Two Mounted Sentries* (1850), p.40 (BL 12602.c.20).

229. PRO WAR 43/1018.
230. PRO WORK 6/24, f.203.
231. The Waterloo medal ribbon is crimson with blue borders on either side.
232. A surviving Waterloo soldier had the initials 'W.M.' (Waterloo Man) in red ink after his name in the regimental records and could claim two years extra service as a gratuity. Their medals, issued early in 1816, were proudly worn by all ranks, and on into civilian life afterwards.
233. P. Egan, *Real Life in London*, (1824).
234. Gold Stick Orders, Household Cavalry Museum.
235. K. de Barri, *The Bucks and Bawds of London Town* (L. Frewin, 1974), p.35.
236. An excellent summary of the creation of the Army numbering process written by Captain A. M. Cherrington, The Life Guards, entitled 'Did you ever wonder who was Number 1?' appears in the Household Cavalry periodical *The Acorn*, Vol. XIX, 1987, pp.52–53.
237. R. Strong, *Lost Treasures of Britain* (Viking, 1990), pp.203–13.
238. R. J. T. Hills, *Something about a Soldier* (London, 1934), p.206.
239. J. H. Stoqueler, *A Personal History of the Horse Guards from 1750 to 1872* (1873), p.180.
240. Stoqueler, *A Personal History of the Horse Guards*, p.194.
241. PRO WAR 43/81
242. Revd A. Barry, *The Life and Works of Sir Charles Barry* (London, 1867).
243. PRO WAR 43/81, 43/104, 40/1805.B.
244. PRO WORK 6/22, 1834.
245. Royal Academy Exhibitors, ref. 1034.
246. PRO WORK 30/185– 196, and Barry, *The Life and Works*.
247. Royal Library, Windsor Castle, Inventory Nos. 18017/18023.
248. E. Longford, *Victoria* (Pan Books, 1964), pp.311–12.
249. Sir R. Biddulph, *Lord Cardwell at the War Office* (John Murray, 1904).
250. W. W. C. Verner, *The Military Life of the Duke of Cambridge* (John Murray, 1905).
251. Banks acting as financial agents to the Army continued to do business in that role at least up to the 1930s; vide H. Gordon, *The War Office* (Putnam, 1935), p.346 n.20.
252. See also G. Rudé, *Some Financial and Military Aspects of the Gordon Riots* (Corporation of London, 1956).
253. De Beer, *Diary of John Evelyn*, p.552, 1 March 1671. The artist Sir Peter Lely charmingly depicted this incident.
254. 33 and 34 Vict. c.17 and Order in Council 4 June 1870.
255. Verner, *The Military Life of the Duke of Cambridge*, Vol. 2, p.402.
256. Ibid., p.411.
257. Ibid., p.416.
258. Ibid., p.440.
259. Ibid., p.442.
260. Ibid., p.446.
261. PRO WAR 43/874 for the War Office move to Pall Mall 1855–56; PRO MPD 158 & 163 for War Office buildings plans 1872–81.
262. 'The Lesson' (1899–1902), Rudyard Kipling. *The Collected Poems of Rudyard Kipling* (Wordsworth, 1994), p.309.
263. e.g. PRO WORK 30,3357, 1910.
264. District Order No.279, 9 Dec 1901. Even allowing for the observations of this history, the Tiltyard Guard and its activities appear to remain a little-known subject; such a study – 'The Foot Guards at Horse Guards' – would surely repay scholarly attention.
265. Arthur, *The Story of the Household Cavalry*, Vol. III, p.6.
266. *Clarke Papers*, Royal Historical Society, 1992, Vol.1, p.22.
267. Gordon, *The War Office*, p.76.
268. LCC, *Survey of London*, Vol. XVI, Part 1, p.178.
269. Pevsner, *The Cities of London and Westminster*, p.538 n;
270. HMC, *Portland*, 1902.
271. Arthur, *The Story of the Household Cavalry*, Vol.III, pp.98–99.
272. Ibid., n. pp.115–16.
273. For fuller details of the 'Red Eagles' see A. Billingham, *America's First Two years* (J. Murray, 1942), also *The Times*, 12 November 1940 and 10 January 1941. For Guards' memoirs, *The Guards Magazine*, Summer 2004, pp.138–9, Winter 2004, p.294.
274. J. N. P. Watson, *Through Fifteen Reigns* (Spellmount, 1997), p.163.
275. *The Times*, 31 January 1949.
276. Vide Watson, *Through Fifteen Reigns*, p.165 et seq. for an excellent account of present-day Household Cavalry service life and responsibilities.
277. See G. Lowthin, *The Eagle* (Minerva, 1999), for full details.
278. See Hogg, 'The Office of Master Gunner', p.91. The original 'Home District' covered London, Berkshire, Buckinghamshire, Middlesex, Surrey and Oxfordshire.
279. R. Alford, *On The Word of Command: A pictorial history of the Regimental Sergeant Major* (Spellmount, 1990), pp.112–22, 'The Garrison Sergeant Majors of Headquarters, London District'.
280. F. H. Cripps-Day, *The Triumph holden at Shakespeare's England* (London, 1912) Guildhall Library S394.7; also *The Times* 10 July 1912, p.11; 12 July 1912, p.8; 20 July 1912, p.11.
281. Arthur, *The Story of the Household Cavalry*, Vol. II, p.467. The 'war' was the Seven Years' War.
282. Ibid., Vol. II, p.468.
283. Ibid., Vol. II, p.468n.
284. The name of the Royal Horse Guards regiment has been subject to more variations than that of any other regiment: for the date shown it was as given here. For details of all the names vide Arthur, *The Story of the Household Cavalry*, Vol. I, p.28.
285. PRO WAR 3/370.
286. R. J. T. Hills, *A Short History of the Life Guards*, p.55.
287. C. T. Atkinson, *History of the Royal Dragoons 1661–1934* (Glasgow University Press, 1934), p.314.
288. Ibid., p.321.
289. Arthur, *The Story of the Household Cavalry*, Vol. II, pp.651–652.
290. Ibid., Vol. III, pp.26–27. See also *The Graphic*, 18 February 1899 for an illustration by the military artist Harry Payne entitled *A Squadron Leader of the Royal Horse Guards halting his men after a Charge*.
291. PRO WAR 2/42, pp.3–9.
292. PRO WAR 26/23, p.309.
293. PRO WAR 43/634 for examples of 'drum beat' recruiting orders.

Index

References to illustrations are shown in **bold**.